BRINGING
IT ALL
BACK HOME

Nuala O'Connor was born and brought up in Dublin and is a graduate of its Trinity College. From 1979 to 89 she worked as a researcher, and later producer, for RTE television and radio. Subsequently she has been researching material for the television series Bringing It All Back Home.

Do Philib á Cheoil

PUBLISHED BY BBC BOOKS,
a division of BBC Enterprises Limited,
Woodlands, 80 Wood Lane, London W12 0TT
First published 1991
© *Nuala O'Connor 1991*
ISBN 0 563 36195 6
Set in 12/14 Bodoni by Butler & Tanner Ltd, Frome, Somerset
Printed and bound in Great Britain by Butler & Tanner Ltd,
Frome, Somerset
Cover printed by Clays Ltd, St Ives PLC, England

BRINGING IT ALL BACK HOME

THE INFLUENCE OF IRISH MUSIC

NUALA O'CONNOR

BBC BOOKS

ACKNOWLEDGEMENTS

I would like to express my gratitude to all those who helped me in the researching and writing of this book.

Firstly to my partner Philip King whose idea it was to make five documentaries which would tell the story of Irish music. His unshakeable belief in the undertaking, his irrepressible enthusiasm and his energy were a constant source of support and encouragement.

I am greatly in the debt of Nicholas Carolan, Administrator of the Irish Traditional Music Archive, who read the manuscript, made corrections, suggested changes, and made the archive accessible to me. To Sadhbh Nic Ionnraic also of the Irish Traditional Music Archive, I am grateful for her help and assistance. For his expert advice and corrections of the text I thank Jackie Small.

Much of this book was written in the Tyrone Guthrie Centre at Annaghmakerrig in County Monaghan. My thanks are due to all the staff there and particularly to Geraldine O'Reilly whose understanding of the subject and insights on many issues provided much needed stimulus.

My thanks also to Jean Ritchie and George Pickow in Port Washington, Long Island, for their warm welcome, gracious hospitality and use of their superb archive. To Mick Moloney in Philadelphia who helped me in many ways, buíochas mór.

For practical advice and help I am indebted to Harry Bradshaw, Peter Browne, Helen Davis, Diane Hamilton, Anne-Louise Kelly, Joan Maguire, Judy Murray, Killian O'Donnell, Rionach Uí Ógáin, Bairbre Ní Fhloinn, Mathias Yauch, and to Heather Holden-Brown, Karen Willie, and Julian Flanders, my enthusiastic and patient editors at BBC Books. Thanks also to Peter Bridgewater for his beautiful book design.

And finally for making it all possible, and for their commitment and generosity I am profoundly grateful to all those musicians who contributed to *Bringing It All Back Home*. Fad saoil agaibh.

Bringing It All Back Home is a five part documentary film series about the journey, influence and development of Irish music. It is a Hummingbird Production for BBC Television in association with RTE. Transmission is scheduled for Spring 1991. A triple album, double cd and cassette of music from the series is also available, catalogue numbers REF 844, BBC CD 844 and ZCD 844.

PICTURE CREDITS

All colour photos © Stephen Meany, specially taken for BBC Enterprises, except the following: Van Morrison © London Features International/Andy Catlin; U2 (top) © Frank Spooner Pictures/Liason, (bottom) © Jim Rakete/Principle Management; Sinéad O'Connor © LFI/Noel Preston, and The Pogues © LFI/G Du Bose.

All b/w pictures © Stephen Meany, specially taken for BBC Enterprises, except the following: page 7 National Library of Ireland, Dublin; 22 The Bettmann Archive; 25 New York Public Library; 28 & 32 Jean Richie/photo George Pickow; 37 The Wilson Collection, Cobh; 38 National Library of Ireland, Dublin; 40 Mary Evans Picture Library; 42 University College Dublin; 46 State Historical Society of Wisconsin; 51 A J Russell; 57 *Puck* magazine; 62 Na Píobairí Uilleann; 64 National Library of Ireland, Dublin; 66 Hulton Picture Company; 69 Mary Evans Picture Library; 79 The Irish Traditional Music Archive, Dublin; 80 Chicago Irish Music Society; 88 Na Píobairí Uilleann; 92 GA Duncan; 94 Lensmen; 105 & 106 Pictorial Press; 108 Roy Esmonde; 117 (bottom) Paul Kolnik/courtesy of Ethnic Folk Arts Centre; 118 GA Duncan; 123 Camera Press; 125 Roy Esmonde; 129 Anton Corbijn; 133 Shanachie Records; 136 Roy Esmonde; 144 (top & bottom) Val Wilmer; 146 LFI; 154 Collections/Brian Shuel; 160 Terry O'Neill; 171 P Chatterton/Virgin Venturi and 173 Catherine Ennis.

Contents

THE DAWNING OF THE DAY

I have a theory that soul music originally came from Scotland and Ireland[1]

VAN MORRISON

For several centuries now Irish music has been on the move, carried in the hands and voices of Irish people. *Bringing It All Back Home* attempts to chart some of its journeys; to go to some of the places reached, and to tell the story of how it inevitably wound its way back home again, as if to bear out that cyclical impulse at the heart of Irish artistic expression, the 'commodious vicus of recirculation' as Joyce thought of it.

The journeys undertaken were physical journeys – to America, England, and to a lesser extent Canada and Australia. These waves of emigration began in the eighteenth century and have not yet receded. America is an important element in the story of *Bringing It All Back Home*. It was in America that the future development of Irish music, including traditional music, and indeed of American folk music, was shaped.

Every living music undertakes a journey through time. But time is relative, and the journey of Irish music through time exemplifies this. On the one hand, traditional music changed very slowly, if at all. The culture it expressed remained much as it always had been ... Irish-speaking, rural, and poor. Time was a commodity in plentiful supply and must have seemed to

1 Van Morrison. Interview,

BIABH

move slowly. So we get long songs of thirty verses and more to accommodate longer memories and an abundance of time. The spirit which animated this culture still lives on in parts of Ireland. As we shall see it was carried through the music into twentieth-century Ireland, changed, but recognisable. But in America, a new country, rapid change was the driving force, and Irish music absorbed this spirit of the new age, in order to re-invent itself, and meet the musical needs of the New World.

The twentieth-century influences of media and technology have sent Irish music off in many different directions, towards rock, country, pop, electric folk, blues, and the avant-garde.

Old collections of the past have also played a part in revitalising contemporary Irish music, particularly the classical tradition.

All of these Irish musical forms are offspring of the same traditional-music parent. They do not all co-exist happily together: some are regarded by others as bastards; some are at loggerheads; some are ignorant of their illustrious parentage. But they do share common features, not necessarily of musical construction, but of spirit, which identify them as Irish.

Through the music, then, that has touched all of these generations, we can read the history of Ireland and her people, especially her emigrant people.

Queenstown, now known as Cobh, Co. Cork. This was the main port of departure for Irish emigrants until the 1950s

The traditional music of Ireland was the only enduring cultural baggage, intangible as it was, that impoverished emigrants could take out of the country.

In the past one hundred and fifty years Ireland has had more of its people leave the country than remain in it. This is unique in the history of emigration.

Being Irish outside Ireland is central to the Irish experience. As sociologist, Liam Ryan, recently wrote: 'Emigration is a mirror in which the Irish nation can see its true face.' The question of identity for Irish people is fraught with ambivalence and tensions. Tensions come in the form of contradictory pressures – one to become assimilated into the new country, the other to affirm exclusive Irishness.

This music inevitably changed in the process of travel, sometimes to be unrecognisably transformed, sometimes evolving at the natural pace dictated by the passing of time and a changing world. In places here and there, often on opposite sides of the globe, it remained almost untouched, a living, vibrant bridge to the past. Nor, as we shall see, was the traffic all one way. Music returned to Ireland in many guises at different times, re-invigorating the tradition when it most needed it, 'Bringing It All Back Home' – to the source and sensibility from which it had sprung.

IRISH MUSIC . . . SOUL MUSIC

Musicians as diverse as Van Morrison and the classically trained, film-score composer Elmer Bernstein have identified a mysterious quality in traditional Irish music. Somehow it has the ability to express the spiritual character of the human psyche in its most profound experiences of love, grief, loneliness, joy in nature, sensuality and celebration. Nowhere is this more evident than in the performance of the music. Mícheál Ó Súilleabháin, a music lecturer at University College Cork, warns that to try to analyse the music without reference to the performance will yield no insights. What makes Irish music unique is the people who make the music: 'The most important thing in music is the technique of making it – and at the heart of the creative process itself – the thing at the heart of the music making, is something which is in the fingers or in the throat technique of the singer.'[2]

He further identifies Ireland's peripheral position in Europe, half in the first world, half in the third world, half

2 Mícheál Ó Súilleabháin,
Interview, BIABH

industrialised, half rural, as influencing the way in which Irish music has evolved. Add to this the fact that Ireland was colonised for eight hundred years, during which time Gaelic culture and language were almost totally wiped out. 'We're linked directly ... here in Ireland into modern audio-visual technology and yet we have this older rural tradition existing in the cities, it's transferred from the country into the city, and instead of actually losing its heart, it started to find something, and it's almost like it's coming home'.[4]

TRADITIONAL MUSIC

There are myriad definitions of the term, 'traditional music', but basic to all of them is the fundamental characteristic of oral transmission. In other words the music is passed on by mouth and by ear not by written word or musical notation. The music is learned from the performances of other singers and players and one generation learns from the next in this manner. As Mícheál Ó Súilleabháin has said: 'Traditional music has to come out of an actual meeting of bodies in space, you know, people communicating; and I think it always has that immediacy and root and warmth as a result.'[5]

Ireland is unique in the western world in still retaining a vigorous, orally transmitted tradition of music. As many attest, this 'warm' musical atmosphere exerts an influence on musicians working outside the pure traditional field. Traditional music has remained uncorrupted by other forms and idioms. It is in no way on the artificial respirator of institutional preservation. It is not a museum piece. It is alive and developing, and involves growing numbers of young musicians – a sure index of health.

On the subject of definitions, the term 'folk' music is often used interchangeably with the term 'traditional' music. However, the two are not necessarily one and the same. In addition to having a 'folk' music tradition which can be described as 'music of the people', Ireland also has two highly developed musical forms. One of these, the harping tradition, now defunct, was never 'folk music'. The second, the 'Sean Nós' tradition, drew some of its elements from mediaeval bardic poetry which was the preserve of a scholarly élite. These forms are as complex and sophisticated as classical or European art music. In their highest forms of expression, they are inaccessible to many performers and listeners.

'That kind of stuff [Irish traditional music] I think comes directly from life ... that kind of music springs directly uncensored from the soul of the people ... it has no intellect that says I'd better do this or I'd better do that; it's soul music if you like.'
ELMER BERNSTEIN[3]

3 Elmer Bernstein.
   Interview, *BIABH*

4 Mícheál Ó Súilleabháin.
   Interview, *BIABH*

5 Ibid

The other characteristic of traditional music is anonymity. There were, and are, composers, but the nature of the music and the performance of it are such that the composer, even if known, is of little significance.

The tune itself, in its original form, is only the barest outline of the melody. If it were to be played in this way it would be incomplete. Consequently, another defining characteristic of traditional music is the degree of variation and ornamentation that occurs in its performance. The execution of the music is heavily dependent on the skill and creative imagination of the player. So within the actual performance itself there is an element of controlled extemporisation. In this way each time a player plays a tune, he plays it as it were for the first time. Each time he plays will be different from the last time. In this way it is rather like jazz. There is, however, a defined musical structure within which this extemporisation is allowed to take place. It is the mastery of this, in addition to imagination and skill, which combine to produce a great player. The player is both performer and composer.

A player who attempts to move outside this structure (a rare occurrence) will not be able to play with other players. The nature of the transmission and performance of the music would work against this happening because Irish traditional music involves a community of musicians. Although exceptionally fine players abound, they are not simply a collection of soloists. A large part of the ethos of Irish traditional playing is players playing together in session for each other. Gigs and paid concert performances are only one small part of the picture. Very few traditional musicians in Ireland make a living out of playing. Until very recently the very idea of a professional traditional musician in the concert performance sense would have been unusual. An intrinsic part of the tradition is that there is no audience as we understand it in the modern sense.

This will become clearer as a concept when we look deeper into the performance aspect of Irish music.

THE ORIGINS OF TRADITIONAL MUSIC

The traditional music of Ireland as we know it today cannot be classified as 'ancient'. We do know, though, that music had an important place in ancient Ireland, important enough to be mentioned in an Irish mythological account of the origins of the three categories of Irish music, the 'suantraí' or lullabies, the 'geantraí' or joyful airs, and the 'goltraí' or laments. These categories are literary inventions, and do not represent any actual classification of Irish music. Significantly a central role in the table is ascribed to a musical instrument, a harp, which has magical powers. Although there is evidence that there were a number of musical instruments in use in ancient Ireland, the harp had pride of place.

The harper was the most elevated of Irish musicians. A feature of Irish society until the demise of the old Gaelic order in the seventeenth century, the harp has retained a symbolic pre-eminence if not a musical one. It is the national emblem on Irish coinage. It is also the logo for Guinness stout.

Because of the oral nature of traditional music we have no idea what this ancient music sounded like. The thread which joined Irish music to its past was largely severed in the seventeenth century, a century which also saw the beginning of the documentation and notation of Irish music.

There is no doubt, though, that some Irish musical forms particularly the 'Sean Nós' singing tradition has an ancient past. 'Sean Nós', in Irish, means the old style.

So if we were to look at the important elements which went into the making of Irish traditional music we would see first of all an ancient Gaelic culture located on the very edge of Europe, more or less unaffected by the imperial predations of the Roman Empire. This culture was assimilated somewhat uneasily into Christianity, maintaining its distinctive features until Norman and then English colonisation began to erode it.

TRADITIONAL MUSIC TODAY

The national repertoire, as it is today, is rooted in the popular music of the seventeenth and eighteenth centuries. It consists of instrumental music, mostly dance music, airs, but also songs in Irish and English, and the musical remnants of the harping tradition of the old Gaelic aristocratic order.

This harping tradition did not survive beyond the eighteenth century. It was an oral tradition and the only way of reconstructing it is by way of eighteenth-century transcriptions of music collected from the last few harpers still playing then.

INSTRUMENTAL MUSIC

Most Irish traditional instrumental music played today is dance music. It is now more usually played for listening to than for dancing. Why this is so will be explained later.

The majority of tunes in a traditional player's repertoire will consist of reels, and jigs, and (depending on their particular regional style, background, learning experience, or taste) of hornpipes, polkas, slides, mazurkas, and highlands. In addition, some musicians, not all, will on occasion, play airs and song airs (the instrumental versions of songs) almost always as solo pieces. These airs are often referred to as 'slow airs' to differentiate them from the rhythmic dance music which is more usually played. A beautiful example of this kind of air is 'A Stór mo Chroí' played by uilleann piper Liam O'Flynn and recorded for *Bringing It All Back Home*. Also recorded for the series was the song version sung by the Keane sisters, Sarah and Rita, of Caherlistrane, Co. Galway, in the west of Ireland.

The traditionally trained uilleann piper Davy Spillane successfully contemporises the slow air, using both pipes and low whistle, and accompaniment (including electric guitar) in his own composition 'Equinox'. He achieves the same mood and ambience of the slow air. There can be no doubt that the source of inspiration for this haunting, ethereal piece of music is deep in the melodic conventions of the playing of airs.

There is one other small category of instrumental music, but one of ancient lineage. These are marching tunes. Clan marches came under interdict in the seventeenth century. Because of their association with the old Gaelic aristocracy they were considered to be seditious. Fortunately for us some of them were deemed too good to give up and were adapted as double jigs for dance music. The harper Máire Ní Chathasaigh recorded one such tune for *Bringing It All Back Home*. It's now a jig called the 'Humours of Ballyloughlin'.

DANCE MUSIC

Dance music can be broken down into roughly seven or eight dance forms. (These are described in more detail in Chapter 5.) Breandán Breathnach, one of the most authoritative scholars of traditional music, estimated as recently as 1985 that the national repertoire of reels, jigs, and hornpipes stood at over 6000 individual pieces, with hundreds more tunes for different kinds of dances like polkas, sets, half sets and so on. It's important to understand that these are living tunes, not tunes which have been collected and noted by folklorists. They are in the repertoire of living, practising musicians.

The different dances are designated by their particular time signature, or metre, or beats to the bar. The unifying principle

of the dance music in performance is known as the 'round'.

The 'round' is described by Mícheál Ó Súilleabháin as 'not a theoretical concept . . . but a feeling of main pulses'. It consists of a thirty-two-bar formula, or thirty-two 'main pulses' within which there are usually two strains or 'parts' of eight bars. Each of these is repeated – 'doubled' in traditional music parlance – to make a total of thirty-two bars. This usually makes up the tune, which is repeated once again from the beginning. This is followed directly by another tune, played in such a way that one flows effortlessly into the other. To the untutored ear it's not always apparent that two tunes have been played. Listening and/or playing are the two ways of recognising the structure, and appreciating the subtleties of the music.

As always, there are exceptions. The parts may be played more than twice, or there may be more than two parts or strains in the tune. The whole will always be broken down into units of eight bars though. If you listen, for example, to the recording of Mary Bergin playing on tin whistle two reels, 'The Blackberry Blossom' and 'Lucky in Love', you will notice that she sticks to the standard formula as outlined above. She plays the first strain twice, then the second strain twice, a total of

The Keane sisters, Sarah and Rita, are traditional singers from Caherlistrane, Co. Galway. Seen here with their niece (left) singer Dolores Keane thirty-two bars; she then repeats the whole tune again making another thirty-two, and then she goes straight into the second reel, 'Lucky in Love', which is played the same way. 'The Blackberry Blossom' is played by Irish fiddler Paddy Glackin with two American virtuoso country fiddlers, Mark O'Connor, and country-music star Ricky Skaggs. Having played the first part twice, instead of going into the second part of 'The Black-berry Blossom', they play the first part twice again, making a thirty-two-bar exposition of the first part of the tune. The second part of the tune is doubled twice also. Then they return to the beginning and do it all over again, before going on into the second reel, 'The Saint Anne's'. Their version is exactly twice the length of Mary Bergin's version, but they have remained within the eight-bar-unit formula.

About these 'main pulses' Mícheál Ó Súilleabháin says: 'You can actually feel them move through your body, and you can see them going through the musician's body, if you watch the body movement, which is very important in all kinds of music.'[6] Once you are aware of this principle of 'main pulses' you will quickly become aware of it in the playing. Listening, watching, and/or playing is the only way to experience it. Understanding it adds immeasurably to the enjoyment of the music.

ORNAMENTATION AND VARIATION

Ornamentation and variation lie at the heart of all traditional playing, and singing. It is through variation, embellishment, and ornamentation that the musician expresses his or her technical skill, imaginative powers, mastery of the form, and ultimately his or her personality.

It would be unthinkable in classical music to alter the musical text of say a Beethoven piano sonata. It must be played as written. The melody line cannot be changed; no notes can be added; the time signature cannot stray from that designated by the composer and so on. In traditional music the opposite is the case. The melody is only a framework, a skeleton which gets its flesh and character from the musicians who play it. This will be different each time it is played. It will never change to the point where it is unrecognisable. These differences are subtle, and the deeper the acquaintance the listener has with the music the more they become apparent. The melody will always be the melody; a reel a reel and a jig a jig, and the tune will always operate within its own particular conventions.

6 Ibid

To variation and ornamentation add intonation and style. Then you get a wealth of musical possibilities and this is what Irish music is all about. These are the treasured qualities which make the tradition so rich and so immensely varied.

SINGING

Two obvious divisions exist in Irish singing: songs in the Irish language and songs in English, and two distinctive styles exist to go with them. Generally speaking, the singing style in Irish is the older of the two, and the English singing style is based on the 'ballad', which is particular to English-language songs, common to both England and America. With the exception of some mediaeval examples of Ossianic lays in Irish no longer in the living tradition, there are hardly any ballads in the Irish language. There are Irish influences in the English ballads sung in Ireland and an Irish style of singing ballads, but the root is English.

SONGS IN IRISH

With the long, slow decline of the Irish language went much of the music of that culture. In this process the song tradition was more vulnerable than the instrumental music. Not having

Traditional Irish meets traditional Appalachian. Irish fiddler Paddy Glackin plays with American country musician Ricky Skaggs in Nashville for *Bringing It All Back Home*

an existence independent of the language as the instrumental music did, it could not accommodate such radical change.

Breandán Breathnach, in *Folk Music and Dances of Ireland* says: 'The decline of the language involved the rejection of the body of folk-song which had its existence in it. Strangely enough the associated airs were also discarded almost in toto.' So while some fragments of song airs, or indeed of instrumental music, became absorbed into the new repertoire, they are merely 'sustained like particles of matter in a stream' and have not been identified in any systematic way; their age and provenance, as Breathnach says, is a matter of speculation only. Luckily the Irish language and its song culture, although still endangered, did not disappear altogether. The country still has a store of songs in Irish and Irish-speaking singers to sing them. These 'native speakers', so called because they come from those parts of Ireland known as the 'Gaeltacht' where Irish is the first language, sing in the 'Sean Nós' style or old style, a subject which is dealt with in detail in Chapter 12. They sing both Irish and English songs in this style. There are also songs in Irish which are not sung in the 'Sean Nós' style, but these are of more recent origin. Describing this singing style the Irish composer, Seán Ó Riada said: 'In approaching that style of singing which is called in Irish, the Sean Nós – the old style – it is best to listen as if we were listening to music for the first time, with a child's new mind; or to think of Indian music rather than European.'[7]

The defining characteristic of the 'Sean Nós' style is that it is solo, unaccompanied singing, a characteristic that it shares with the European ballad style. 'Sean Nós' singing never, however, developed along the lines of ballad singing which came to incorporate harmony, group singing, and accompaniment. It is now more commonly sung in this manner. 'Sean Nós' remains oral in its method of transmission. So it is a very pure, old, primitive form of singing. It is also a fiendishly difficult and complex form to master, and its best performers are rightly acclaimed as artists of unsurpassing excellence.

It is perhaps the most 'Irish' of Irish musical forms. For this reason where the Irish language did not survive it died out. Nor, unlike the resilient instrumental music, did it survive beyond one generation in America. It is easy to see why the 'Sean Nós' song and the singer who breathes life into it, carry such a precious cultural cargo. 'Sean Nós' involves the transmission of the pure spirit of an ancient and timeless cultural message. The acclaimed traditional musician, Tony

7 Seán Ó Riada, *Our Musical Heritage* (Funduireacht an Riadaigh, 1982), p. 23

MacMahon, speaks of the 'intensely lyrical line' of 'Sean Nós' singing, and is of the opinion that: 'traditional singing in the Irish language is at the centre of our music'.

SONGS IN ENGLISH

The process of British colonisation in Ireland went hand in hand with the demise of Irish as the spoken language of the people.

According to Breandán Breathnach so few Irish songs made a successful transition into English that 'one may deduce a rule that folk songs do not pass from one language to another'.[8]

In musical terms the change-over from Irish to English meant adopting the English ballad, and by ballad we mean a narrative song or poem. (Again there are problems of definition, and there are songs which will fall outside this category, e.g. nonsense songs, lullabies, work songs, carols etc.) There are straightforward 'imports' from England to Ireland – songs like 'Barbara Allen' and 'Little Musgrave'. But folk songs did not die with the demise of Irish, and there also began a tradition of new songs composed in the new language, English.

Often these new songs were written to existing airs which were borrowed from many sources, English, Scottish, or Irish. This is a practice which has continued down to the present day, as anyone familiar with the songs of Bob Dylan, for example, will know.

Not every singer made so free and easy with Irish airs though. The nineteenth-century Irish writer William Carelton tells in his autobiography how his mother, a fine singer, did not like to sing English songs to Irish airs. When requested to sing such a song she replied: 'I'll sing it for you, but the English words and the air are like quarrelling man and wife; the Irish melts into the tune, but the English doesn't.'

Very often these songs in English were printed as 'broadsheets' to be sold in the streets by itinerant ballad singers and travelling people who also sang at fairs, races and other events. There were local songs, old songs, new songs printed on the broadsheets which by all accounts enjoyed a brisk trade. People bought the broadsheet to learn the song, and thus it passed into the folk song repertoire. Sometimes these songs endured for a very long time and became classics. Sometimes they perished and were forgotten, like the ephemeral pop songs of today.

'You have to see the traditional ballads in Ireland in an international English language context, I think, to understand them.' MÍCHEÁL Ó SÚILLEABHÁIN[9]

8 Breandán Breathnach, *Folk Music and Dances of Ireland* (Mercier Press, Cork, 1971)

9 Mícheál Ó Súilleabháin. Interview, *BIABH*

CLASSICAL MUSIC

Ireland has no classical-music tradition in the European art-music sense. As the Irish classically trained composer Seán Ó Riada pointed out, Ireland has a highly developed and complex music which, just because it was orally transmitted, should not be considered solely as 'folk music'. He often made the parallel between this kind of music and the equally highly developed music of oriental cultures, also orally transmitted.

Into these 'classical' categories can be admitted 'Sean Nós' singing, hailed by Irish musicologist and composer Seoirse Bodley as: 'one of the greatest achievements of the Irish people in traditional music and is also superbly complex music in its own right. Using the simplest of means, voice alone, it can demand of the singer the greatest artistry.'

The other category is the instrumental music of the old Irish harping tradition, which was the music of the Irish aristocracy, both native Irish and those descended from the first Anglo-Norman colonisation of Ireland. This latter class had become so intermarried with native Irish stock that, in a much vaunted historical cliché, they became 'more Irish than the Irish themselves'.

This absorption of Irish culture involved the patronage of harpers who were the equivalent of court musicians. It is recorded that Queen Elizabeth I had an Irish harper at her court by the name of Dónal Buidhe.

The harp itself figured as an instrument of importance in ancient Irish legend. There is documentary evidence of its existence in Ireland from the eighth century. There was also a standard Irish harp of distinctive make and style with its own repertoire.

The harpers composed for their patrons special pieces of music, of sophisticated and complex construction. Sadly most of this music is lost to us. We do know that the harps were metal-strung and that the harper played with his nails grown long for the purpose. The sound quality obviously was nothing like that achieved by the gut- and nylon-strung 'Irish' harps of today which the modern harpist plays with the flesh of the fingers. You can read more about the harp and its music in Chapter 12.

In a way the tradition contained the seeds of its own destruction, dependent as it was for its existence on a class whose days were numbered if complete colonisation was to be achieved. The realisation of that objective meant dispossession or surrender.

The option to go down-market and become a folk musician was not really an option. The music of the harpers was incomprehensible to those outside the old order. So it faded away and with it went at least a thousand years of a great tradition.

THE SPIRIT OF THE MUSIC

The idea of journey is a recurring theme in the history of Irish music and with this idea of journey goes its expressed perception of exile. This is especially true of the music. Why leaving the home place should be invariably conceived of as exile, even when it presaged an improvement in life, is bound up with the pre-eminence of landscape in Irish minds and hearts.

Traditional musician Tony MacMahon plays accordion at a house dance in Co. Clare

There is even a word in Irish for it, 'dinnseanchas', meaning literally the lore of place names, but referring also to the ancient practice of writing poems and songs in praise of place. The Irish poet Seamus Heaney is a contemporary 'dinnseanchas' poet for whom this cast in the Irish mind marks Ireland as more than a geographical country but a 'country of the mind'.

It is easier to leave the geographical country than the interior landscape, and many Irish 'exiles' never did. Heaney says: 'This love of place and lamentation against exile from a cherished territory is another typical strain in the Celtic sensibility.'[10] This image of exile can also operate as perceived internal exile; the feeling that for historical reasons the Irish person is a stranger in his own land, and the longing to 'come back' is often articulated in music.

Preoccupation with and love for landscape, feelings of loneliness, and the force of memory, came through again and again in the making of *Bringing It All Back Home* amongst musicians in Ireland, England and America and not only in the area of traditional music.

Tony MacMahon, the accordion player from Co. Clare, spoke eloquently of:

The old feelings; the belief that rocks and rivers and mountains are inhabited by spirits – they're not just shapes – they're three dimensional beings ... and I think that that tune ['Port na bPúcaí, a slow air] is a lonely way of bringing that out, which is the reason I like to play it.

10 Seamus Heaney, 'The God in the Tree. Early Irish Nature Poetry', *Preoccupations – Selected Prose 1968–1978* (Faber & Faber, 1984)

Máire Ní Bhraonáin of the group, Clannad:

> *You know that when we've made an album ... the judgement day for me is when I'm going home to Donegal and ... I put the cassette on then, and if I feel it's worthy of the area, then I'm happy with it ... so that's how I judge my music ... I love going home to Donegal; it is definitely the sole inspiration of Clannad in the long run.*

And finally to Kentucky-born country musician Ricky Skaggs:

> *Well this is my theory.... I feel the Irish tunes had a happy lilt ... and those tunes were brought over to America years and years ago and it seems as if those first or second generation children that grew up playing those tunes started missing their homeland and missing their folks. There was a sadness and a pining and a lonesomeness that just seemed to enter the music, and you know when your heart's broken ... you're gonna play from your heart, you're gonna play much more lonesome feelings and to me that's where that Appalachian Mountain, that High Lonesome Sound ... came into being.*[11]

11 Ricky Skaggs.

Interview, *BIABH*

CHAPTER TWO

THAT HIGH LONESOME SOUND

But the rents were getting higher

and we could no longer stay,

So farewell unto you

Bonny, bonny, Slieve Gallion Braes.

These are the last lines of the song 'Slieve Gallion Braes', sung for *Bringing It All Back Home* by Dolores Keane with her husband John Faulkener and sister Christine.

Slieve Gallion is a mountain in Co. Tyrone in the north of Ireland, an area which became, after the partition of the country in 1921, part of the state of Northern Ireland. It is a place of great beauty lovingly described in the song:

> *As I went a roaming one morning in May*
> *To view the fair valleys and mountains so gay*
> *I was thinking of the flowers all doomed to decay*
> *That bloom around ye bonny, bonny Slieve Gallion Braes.*

The story behind the song is that of the overwhelming emigration from this part of Ireland in the eighteenth century. The inhabitants of this area, mostly small farmers, were Presbyterians of Scottish stock and relatively recently arrived at that. Most of them had settled in this province of Ireland, during the so-called Ulster Plantation of the seventeenth century.

In some respects they resembled the older Catholic native Irish, having come from the same kind of agricultural economy with similar traditions.

Like the native Irish they suffered religious persecution. In the eighteenth century this, together with economic distress caused by bad harvests and high rents, combined to push them out. . . . These people made up the first mass Irish migration to America. Their going had an impact on the subject matter of song making in Ireland long after they had been absorbed into American society. A huge store of Irish emigration songs date from this time. They settled in the Appalachian mountain regions of east-coast America. They were known as the Scots-Irish and the music and songs they brought with them were subsumed into American folk music. 'They brought with them aspects of a culture which were eventually to mutate into what's now known as Appalachian old-time music, song and dance.'

This Appalachian sound would go on to play a role in the making of a quintessential American music: rock 'n' roll.

Appalachian mountain country. Birthplace of 'That High Lonesome Sound'

EXODUS

The rents were getting higher,
and we could no longer stay.

Not only were rents getting higher, but eighteenth-century Ulster was characterised by an unjust and repressive landlord-tenant system.
In 'Slieve Gallion Braes' the singer leaves us in no doubt:

It's not for the want of employment at home,
That caused all the sons of old Ireland to roam,
But those tyrannising landlords,
They would not let us stay
So farewell unto ye
Bonny, bonny Slieve Gallion Braes.

The system of land-owning in Ireland was characterised by a high degree of absenteeism; one third or more of land-owners lived in Britain and saw their estates and hapless tenants as a source of income and nothing else. Very few invested in improvements and preferred to make money by increasing rents. By 1711 the average annual rent of an acre of Irish land was equivalent to the purchase price of an acre of land in America. Once people became aware of better conditions abroad they were provided with a powerful incentive to leave. The sentiments of many emigrants of this time are expressed in another Ulster song, 'The Rambling Irishman':

But to live poor, I could not endure,
Like others of my station,
To Amerikay I sailed away,
And left this Irish nation.

Whole congregations and communities moved *en masse* to escape religious persecution. America was seen as a country where the liberty to worship in freedom would be guaranteed, and where the means to support a decent standard of living could be maintained. This mass movement often took the form of a pastor leading his whole flock out to the new country, taking with them farm implements, and seeds for planting (and their singing tradition and music).

It is chilling to imagine the social disruption caused as the homesteads of whole parishes were sold up and deserted. It's not surprising that songs of emigration which recount the events of that time are still sung. For most of the eighteenth century seventy-five per cent of Irish emigrants were Protestants. Nearly three quarters of these were Presbyterians. The rest were Anglicans, Quakers and other Protestant denominations.

From a country in which the overwhelming population was Catholic, this represented an enormous number of people. Somewhere between 200 000 and 300 000 Protestants emigrated during the first seventy-five years of the eighteenth century.

Davy Hammond is a Belfast man, a singer and a film producer. He has made many programmes about the music and song culture of Northern Ireland. According to Davy these early Presbyterian emigrants were as aesthetically involved with their landscape as their Catholic neighbours and 'mourned very grievously for the place they left, and these emigration songs are always about that ... about leaving the hills and the fields and the small streams'. For them 'the landscape was very informative. It charged their emotional life and their imagination.'

AMERICA - LAND OF LIBERTY

It is true to say that there was no homogenous Protestant migration. Some emigrants were well-to-do and certainly not leaving under compulsion of poverty or persecution. Neither was the migration uniformly rural. There were tradesmen and town dwellers. Nevertheless most of those who left were from rural backgrounds, small-holdings at that. Some of them were forced by poverty to offer themselves as indentured servants in return for the passage money. This was *de facto* slavery. Indentureship was a system whereby the person wishing to emigrate signed himself over usually to the shipmaster for a stipulated term. The shipmaster then sold his services as a servant on the other side. Another way was to sign on with a better-off farmer who needed farm workers in America and become his indentured servant. The ultimate goal was to serve the time, finish the indenture and then buy some land. Land-ownership would have been beyond the means of rack-rented tenantry in Ulster.

Their aspirations were traditional. Ambition and self-interest had not yet been made virtues of.

America was seen as a place where there was ample land, no landlords, no rents, and where a family could be supported in comfort.

The pattern of settlement of this migration was diverse, spread as it was over a wide area of America and including cities and towns. The particular settlement that is of interest in the story of *Bringing It All Back Home* is that of the Appalachian Scots or Scots-Irish. There in the Appalachian mountain country of Virginia, West Virginia, Kentucky, Tennessee, North and South Carolina, Irish music evolved into what has become known as 'That High Lonesome Sound'.

The singing tradition brought by the Scots-Irish was English-language balladry for the most part. This would have meant unaccompanied solo singing at that time. Some of the ballads would have come from Scotland and England. There would also have been songs of more recent local composition. According to the late song collector, Seán O'Baoill: 'the two main tributaries, Scots and English, flow into the main Irish stream of Ulster folk song. Ever since the Battle of Kinsale in 1601, there has been a constant interchange of songs between Ireland and Britain'.[1]

English and Scots ballads were adapted to Irish airs if considered to be superior, and idioms used by song makers and poets in the Irish language found their way into new ballads in English. There were songs in Irish in abundance, but with the decline of the language in Ulster many of these songs and

Immigrants awaiting processing at Ellis Island, New York, 1910

1 Seán O'Baoill, 'Traditional Singing in English – The Ulster Dimension', *Treoir*, Feb. 1974, p. 8.

some of the airs disappeared. It is not always possible at this remove to be specific about the origins of individual songs because as Seán O'Baoill says, 'the traditions so overlap and intertwine that it's impossible to dogmatise about the origins of some songs either in words or in music'.[2]

Certainly there was and is a distinct singing tradition in Ulster. Davy Hammond typifies this style as one where 'the music would run to a more rhythmic line, [and] you wouldn't have the same number of grace notes or decorations [as in the rest of Ireland]'. That this tradition travelled with emigrants to America is not in doubt. In some cases, the songs even remained exactly the same as when they left.

Seán O'Baoill instances the example of a Scots ballad 'The Knight on the Road' which he recorded from a traditional singer in Co. Tyrone in the fifties. The melody was an air known as the 'The Uist Tramping Song'. Before this two living versions of the song had been recorded, one unsurprisingly in the Highlands of Scotland; the other in the Appalachian mountains in the thirties. He reckoned that it had been known in Ulster for over two hundred years. The Ulster, or Scots-Irish element in Appalachia was well established by the end of the eighteenth century. Kerby Miller estimates that '50% or more of the settlers on the trans-Appalachian frontier were of Ulster lineage'.[3] Here they met other settlers of English, Swedish and German extraction. Over generations they intermarried, founded communities, until eventually it became impossible to identify an 'Ulster American' community as such.

The American ethnomusicologist Alan Lomax has written of the musical interaction of these early settlers:

> *The Southern mountains preserved the traditional ballads, lyric songs, and dance tunes in comparative isolation, thus permitting the emergence of hybrid songs, which were on the one hand fusions of Scots, Irish and English influences and on the other genuine reflections of pioneer culture patterns.*[4]

'AS I ROVED OUT . . . OLD KING COLE' IN COUNTY ARMAGH

Jean Ritchie is a traditional singer from Viper, in Perry County, south-eastern Kentucky, now living in Long Island, New York. She comes from a long line of singers of 'mountain music' and has written a wonderful account of those early days at home

2 Ibid., p. 8

3 Kerby Miller, *Emigrants and Exiles – Ireland and the Irish Exodus to North America* (OUP, 1985), p. 161

4 John and Alan Lomax, *Best Loved American Folk Songs* (Grosset and Dunlop, 1947), Preface

with her family in *Singing Family of The Cumberlands*. Jean has a huge store of songs which were she says:

> *handed down from the old people. They came from Scotland, England and Ireland, Wales maybe. My father's name was Ritchie and my mother's name was Hall ... she was English and he was Scottish, and there were a lot of Irish, Welsh, and a few German families, and we all got intermarried so that the music got sort of intermarried too; ... so in Kentucky there's a great melting pot of all those countries' music.*[5]

Jean was born in 1922, the last of fourteen children. Her elder brothers and sisters remembered a time before the railroad had come, when 'there weren't even any instruments — we didn't even have a dulcimer ... in the old days they just sang, they didn't have any accompaniment to their voice.' This style of singing would have been much the same as traditional singing in Ireland and Britain, melodic and unaccompanied. Unlike the mother tradition there was some unison singing.

As Jean mentioned there were few instruments. Partly this was because of a religious prejudice against musical instruments as 'instruments of the devil' and partly because of lack of availability.

However, the dance tunes did not die out either. They became incorporated into 'play songs':

> *When you danced and you didn't have a fiddle ... you made the rhythm with your hands and you just sang the song, and the people who weren't dancing would stand on the side and help sing and help do the rhythm.*

There were the old ballads like 'Barbara Allen' and lullabies, and 'just any kind of song you can think of.'

Later on came big changes, the railroad in 1911, then coal-mining, the first music recordings, and finally the radio. All these were to change a way of life that had gone on more or less undisturbed for two hundred years. It was to change the music in many ways too.

In 1952 Jean received a Fulbright scholarship to research the origins of some of the Ritchie family's music in the British Isles. With her went her husband George Pickow who was photographer and sound recordist for the expedition. Initially she planned to visit England, Scotland and Wales only. When

5 Jean Ritchie. Interview.

BIABH

Jean Ritchie (right) with
traditional singer
Elizabeth Cronin in Co.
Cork, 1952

she told her English supervisor, a professor at London University, that folk music was the subject of her research, he told her she must go to Ireland. And so, 'We started in Ireland and we spent a long time there, longer than in any other country because we fell in love with the people and with the music.'

She did not have long to wait before she made a connection with her musical 'roots'. It happened in the kitchen of Sara Makem, a traditional singer, who lived in the little town of Keady, Co. Armagh.

> *I have a wonderful recording of her getting supper or tea for us while she's singing and talking to us ... she's singing, you can hear the knife go through the bread – rar! rar! rar! – and you can hear the bacon sizzling. All the time she's singing 'As I roved out on a May morning, on a May morning right early'.*
>
> *I kept listening to it and smelling the bacon and being reminded of something ... it was a play game that we played back home; it was called 'Old King Cole was a Jolly Old Soul' and it used almost the same tune as she was using. So that's how the music got there! Sometimes the words were changed but the tune remained the same. They had a way of keeping the Irish tunes mostly because Irish tunes were far superior, of course!*[6]

Her journey was full of such discoveries, but this one she cherishes dearly: 'she sings her little song and it's so pretty, and it's one of my most treasured recordings; it's nothing you could ever put on a record or anything but I listen to it and I'm reminded of that lovely day'. That song 'As I Roved Out', was, as it happened, very well known to listeners to a folk music programme of the same name, on BBC radio in the late forties and fifties. A fragment of the song sung by Sara was the signature tune.

Tommy Makem, Sara's son who began his musical career with the Clancy Brothers told us a touching story about this same tune and its effect on a man from his and Sara's home town of Keady. This man was

> *away in Africa somewhere ... and he had broken his leg or something; he was in hospital anyway, and he was feeling very sad for himself ... He turned on his radio on Sunday morning [to the BBC World Service] and there was Sara Makem singing. He told me (and he was a big strong man) that he broke down and cried because it brought something of home to him.*

FROM COLERAINE, CO. DERRY, TO MULENBERG COUNTY, KENTUCKY

In 1811 the Irish collector Edward Bunting noted down a song called 'Rosey Connolly' from a singer in Coleraine, Co. Derry, in Northern Ireland. He also noted that the author and the date were unknown. He published the song tune in his 1840 collection, *The Ancient Music of Ireland* and this is the extent of the information we have about 'Rose(y) Connolly' in Ireland except for a text of the song taken down in 1929 by a collector, from a singer in Co. Galway. The words identify the song as a murder ballad. The unfortunate Rose(y) is killed by her lover. Although no reason is given the subtext is probably that of a pregnant girl whose lover is unwilling to face the consequences.

The late American scholar D. K. Wilgus who researched the origins of 'Rose Connolly' outlined the connection between it and a more famous Irish song 'Down by the Salley Gardens'. The words of the song were written by the Irish poet W. B. Yeats. He adapted the lyrics from a song he had heard sung in his youth by an old woman in Co. Sligo.

Down by the salley gardens my love and I did meet.

A willow tree in Ireland is also known as a salley tree. The other name by which Rose Connolly is known in America is 'Down in the Willow Garden':

Down in a Willow Garden
Where me and my love did meet

All Phil Everly of the Everly Brothers knows about the song is that: 'It always just seemed to be there ... the song was one of those traditional songs that people would sing,' while his brother Don commented, 'Our father had a big song book and he had the lyrics to hundreds and hundreds of songs and he knew them all and, you know, we were never smart enough to ask him where he found them.'[7]

Although they never thought about it much, there was an unconscious assumption on their part that the origin of much of the music which they played was Irish, Scottish or English:

> *I think you can really see the influence of Irish music in*
> *the harmonics, at least in the harmony singing ... there's*
> *a lot of fifths and what I call 'spreads' in Irish fiddle*
> *playing and you can hear that, and in the pipes too, you*
> *can hear those spreads.*

On this, as on previous occasions, when they have performed 'Rose Connolly', Phil and Don like to be accompanied by Irish uilleann pipe-player Liam O'Flynn, whom they first met in Ireland some years ago.

They were disappointed to find no trace of an Irish Everly on their first trip there in the fifties: 'Everyone sort of assumed we were Irish anyway ... but the name Everly is not in Ireland ... we had heard that the name was O'Everly, like "Of Everly" and when we got to Ireland they said "Well, sorry" ... We tried very hard to be Irish.'

Phil and Don's background is Mulenberg county, Kentucky, although they spent most of their youth in Shenendoah, Iowa. Their father, like the rest of the community in Mulenberg county had begun his working life, at a young age, working in the coal-mine, after which he left to work as a professional musician, first in Chicago, in a nightclub. He eventually moved to Iowa where he had his own radio show on which Don and Phil joined him as soon as they were able to sing.

So unlike Jean Ritchie who grew up singing as part of a family tradition to provide their own entertainment, the

7 Don and Phil Everly.

Interview. *BIABH*

Everlys were part of the new phenomenon of radio. Don and Phil had the unusual experience as children of going to the radio station every morning to sing on a live show before school. They did maintain contact with their Kentucky roots and they still do. As children they would sing on the porch with the family as Jean Ritchie did. In addition to songs like 'Down in the Willow Garden' they would now sing songs popularised on the radio ... 'cos we were trying to be, you know, Hank Williams and Lefty Frizell and whatever else we could hear'. They went on from those porch try-outs to become stars in their own right and recorded a string of hits in the sixties. They combined the country harmonies they had learned as children with a contemporary rhythmic base to produce a unique Everly Brothers' sound.

This comes through on the old folk song 'Down in the Willow Garden' as much as it does on the waltz time 'Darling don't let our Love Die' (a hit for a thirties' singing group) which was also recorded on the *Bringing It All Back Home* session in Nashville.

RADIO, RAILROADS AND COALMINES

It is hard to underestimate the impact radio had on those communities in the Appalachians and on their music. Before that music had been local ... many of the communities were isolated and inaccessible. The radio had been preceded by the first commercial recordings and the arrival of the record-player, 'Victrola' or 'talkin machine' as it was referred to in Jean Ritchie's youth.

Jean recalls her father ordering a Victrola, from a mail-order catalogue, and travelling a couple of days' journey with a sled and mule to collect it from the depot. It was an object of wonder and amazement wherever he played it. This was the first such machine in Viper.

The radio followed soon after, and this caused even more consternation, particularly because of the kind of music being played. What was taking place was: 'The transformation of Southern white music from its "folk" (or non commercial) origins into the music associated with the term "hillbilly" '.[8] As Jean's mother saw it, it was 'pure devil music ... all these instruments and this rhythm'.

Initially the difference was not in the tunes or songs themselves; it was in the way they were played and sung. Gradually the emphasis shifted, from one or two instrumental performers

From Brownie, to Iowa, to Knoxville, to Nashville, to Hollywood to England and around the world...

Don and Phil have taken the music of Kentucky, as taught by their parents. And now they are bringing it back home to Central City.

August 25, 1988

Plaque to the Everlys in their home town of Central City, Kentucky

8 Earl V. Spielman, 'Traditional North American Fiddling', Ph D thesis (University of Wisconsin, Madison, 1975), p. 244

Jean Ritchie recording
piper Seamus Ennis in
Ireland, 1952

playing together, to bands. Groups of musicians and singers played together, with mandolins, guitars, autoharps, fiddles and banjos backing them. The music was catchy, and included harmonies and backing arrangements hitherto unheard of in the playing and singing of traditional music and song.

> *Prior to radio and phonograph recordings, songs and dances were performed unselfconsciously. There was little concern for arrangement, aesthetic production, or tonal balance, and practically no concern at all about the total length of a performance.*[9]

The radio changed all this. It had a profound effect on the musical life of America. In Appalachia it created the professional 'folk' musician.

Professional musicians were not unknown. They worked in vaudeville, and in travelling shows. But the music of country people in America as in Ireland had always been made by themselves, as in Jean Ritchie's young days. Radio was now replacing the home entertainers. Because of radio, a musician

9 Ibid., p. 246

like Ike Everly was given an alternative to working all his life in a coalmine: 'Dad played guitar and that guitar got him to Chicago, and of course ... we had a better chance at life,' said Phil Everly. Coalmining, following hard on the railroad, spelt another disruption in Kentucky. Initially it meant steady work and a better living than subsistence farming could provide. In the end it meant polluted rivers and land, strip-mining, worked-out mines and economic collapse. Jean Ritchie has written many songs about the impact of the coalmine on her part of Kentucky. Some of these songs have travelled around the world and entered the repertoire of contemporary folk singers.

'The L and N Don't Stop Here Anymore' is a song Jean wrote about a railway line which stopped running when the coal ran out. Recently it was recorded by singer-songwriter Michelle Shocked, and more recently by an Irish singer-songwriter Tony Small. Tony never actually heard Jean's recording but learned the song from an English folk singer in Germany! This is one of the true hallmarks of the authentic folk song – its ability to travel and become part of a network of oral transmission.

In this way commercial recordings or learned versions of them renew the store of contemporary folk songs. True folk song can be depended upon to be recognised for what it is. As Elmer Bernstein says: 'I think you can tell what's a real folk song and what's a phony, because the real ones do have the soul of the people in them.'

'Paradise' is a song written by John Prine about the devastation wrought by strip-mining in Kentucky. He recorded it for *Bringing It All Back Home* at the Nashville sessions.

With the Everlys John shares family roots in Mulenberg County. Like Don and Phil's father, John's parents headed for Chicago to work and rear their family. Like the Everlys they went back regularly to the old hometown, 'Paradise' – a supremely ironic name in the light of what later happened there.

To clear the way for strip-mining the entire town of Paradise was demolished. Today the area has changed beyond all recognition: 'Actually,' says Don Everly, 'if I remember correctly you used to drive uphill to Mulenberg from Nashville – now you drive kind of down.'

The Depression of the thirties forced many rural people from the Appalachians and other parts of the south to move out, to cities or other areas. By doing so they extended the audience for country music. Although the recording industry was in a decline for much of the thirties, radio expanded, and networked radio broadcast country music nationwide. 'Network radio sought to reach and develop a national audience, and therefore attempted to reduce many of the local and regional differences. In music especially, radio contributed to a homogeneity of styles.'[10]

All music was grist to radio's mill. In radio many musical influences came together – jazz, blues, ragtime, cowboy songs, cajun, mariachi, in combination with white Anglo-Saxon traditional music. The outcome of this interaction was to be seen in the string bands and singing groups, in the bluegrass, Texas swing and singing cowboys of the next two decades.

All looked to the traditional source for tunes and sounds. They mixed them with outside musical influences, producing new songs and material with which their particular band or group was then identified. Radio entailed a never-ending demand for material. The entire traditional repertoire was used to supply the demand as was every other musical form available. Later on, rock 'n' roll, electrification of instruments and pop had a levelling effect on these hybrids. In an attempt to sound 'poppy' and 'rocky' much country music became bland and featureless by adopting the worst characteristics of formula pop and rock. Much of what came to be regarded as the 'Nashville sound' fitted into this category and its influence spread beyond Nashville. Fortunately, what rock 'n' roll and pop did was not all bad news for country music. Rock 'n' roll was, after all, born in the south.

Some of this early 'hillbilly' or 'oldtimey' music of the early radio days took root in odd corners of the world, including Ireland. The Lee Valley String Band in Cork in the south of Ireland is a case in point. They play a mixture of traditional and oldtimey material in the style of the singing and instrumental groups of the twenties and thirties. The instrumental line-up is fiddle, banjo, mandolin, autoharp, and guitar. Songs come from sources like the Carter family and Bill Monroe. Matt Cranitch is a traditional musician and fiddle player with the Lee Valley. A meeting with a fiddler from Nashville passing through Cork provided him with an introduction to the music of the Appalachians. It was a mutually fruitful meeting: 'He asked me to show him a few reels and I said I will if you show me a few tunes, and I did, and he did and here I am playing with these lads.'

Back home again!

CHAPTER THREE

THE STRANGER'S LAND

Sorrow filled me leaving Ireland

when I was powerful,

so that mournful grief came to me

in the foreign land.

When emigration began to feature as a fact of life for Irish people, the Irish psyche was disposed to internalise it as exile. The circumstances in which the Irish emigrant departed were famine in the mid-nineteenth century, and rural poverty or stagnation in later years. This, coupled with the colonial status of Ireland, added to the sense of enforced exile. It was reflected in a tradition of emigration songs which is now three hundred years old. It is, though, a tradition which has its roots in the earliest poetry of Gaelic Ireland.

A monastic poet of the twelfth century put the words shown above in the mouth of the sixth-century saint, Colum Cille (founder of the city of Derry in Northern Ireland).

The theme of enforced exile from the much loved home place, accompanied by an almost pagan celebration of nature, are continuous threads through Irish poetry and song. The sentiments expressed in this twelfth-century poem would have struck the hearts of Irish listeners down through the centuries. The beauty of the poem, its unsentimental yet emotional expressiveness are also characteristic of a particular genre of Irish songs of exile.

The poem goes on to praise the places the saint loves, displays a great joy in nature, and finishes on a note of bitter regret and longing for home:

> *I have loved the lands of Ireland, I speak truth; it would be delightful to spend the night with Comgall and visit Canice.*[2]

They are leaving old Ireland No longer can stay, And thousands are sailing to Amerikay.[1]

Successive centuries of invasion and colonisation – Viking, Norman, and English – brought about consciousness of an internal exile. Many Irish saw themselves as 'strangers in their own land', dispossessed, suffering under the tyranny of foreigners.

Feelings of exile and dispossession were not universal. They were dependent, to some degree, on time and place. Where colonisation was successful and where English became the spoken language of the native Irish, the old ways were forgotten. As the Irish poet Thomas Kinsella says: 'The loss was not regretted in English-speaking Ireland, in so far as it was felt at all.'[3]

IRISH MIGRATION BEFORE THE FAMINE

1 Emigration song, 'Thousands are Sailing'

2 Colum Cille, *A Golden Treasury of Irish Poetry*, ed. David Greene and Frank O'Connor (Macmillan, London, 1967)

3 Thomas Kinsella, Introduction, *New Oxford Book of Irish Verse* (OUP, 1986), p. xxv

The first Catholic Irish emigrants to reach America were not as is often supposed victims of the Famine of the 1840s. For a full century and more before that, they had been coming to America as transported convicts and indentured servants, sometimes kidnapped for the purpose, so high was the demand for labour in the colonies. They met prejudice and ill treatment. Many, unable to withstand the climatic conditions, died of tropical diseases. It was soon realised that black slave-labour was more suited to the purpose and the experiment in white Irish slave-trading did not last long.

Otherwise Irish Catholic emigrants tended to be either adventurer members of the lower gentry, artisans or itinerant labourers. The majority were males travelling alone. They tended to disappear into the American hinterland without establishing themselves in any kind of ethnically focused Irish community.

The nineteeth century in Ireland saw many changes. The first and most obvious one was the explosion in population growth from four million in 1780 to seven million in 1821. There was also an increase in the use of English and in literacy in that language. Communications and transport improved, and restrictions on travel out of the country were lifted. The pace of emigration picked up and Catholics began to outnumber Protestant emigrants. The 'American letters' began to arrive. These were letters sent home by emigrants to relatives, and usually contained money. Indeed the 'American letter' was a synonym for money. If the letter contained no money, no one advertised the fact. The letter more often than not contained the passage money for another member of the family. In 1838 fifty per cent of Irish emigrants' fares were paid by family members already living in America. Initially the popular route was by sail from Liverpool to New York, the fare costing between two and three pounds. From the mid-1820s poorer people began to make up the numbers of those emigrating, numbers which increased or were maintained at a high level from then on.

Emigration to Britain in this period also increased and indeed for poorer Irish people who could not afford the fare to America, Britain was preferred. The fare for a channel crossing was ten pence or less. Between 1830 and 1835, 200 000 Irish people left for Britain. The ranks of Irish emigrants in Liverpool were swelled by numbers of Irish who had set out for the first leg of the journey to America. Having been fleeced of all their money by unscrupulous ticket-brokers and inn-keepers, they were forced to stay in Liverpool. These Irish immigrants, destitute and unskilled, found themselves at the bottom of the social ladder in English cities, living in slums, employed if at all in lowly paid occupations.

By now there was also a long-established pattern of seasonal migration from the north and west of Ireland to Scotland, and from the south and east of Ireland to London and the English Midlands. These migrants would have included families travelling together to work in the textile industry, or men looking for work as navvies.

The Ireland they were leaving behind was one in which it was becoming harder to maintain even a subsistence standard of living. Fierce competition for land was forcing rents up to unaffordable levels. Smallholders could not afford improvements like drainage or fertiliser, so their land was inefficiently used. The practice of dividing up a family holding into smaller and smaller plots between members was putting intolerable pressure on the land to produce enough to keep families fed.

Tender leaving Queenstown, Co. Cork, at the turn of the century. Glasgow was a popular destination for migrant workers

The potato was a crop which yielded well and was nutritious. Supplemented by buttermilk, eggs, or fowl, it provided a fairly healthy diet. By the late 1840s the struggle to pay rent had engulfed smallholders, cottiers, and landless labourers. Seventy-five per cent of the rural population of Ireland was totally dependent on the potato as the sole source of food. When potato stocks ran low before the harvest, destitution and near-starvation were commonplace. In spite of this, music-making was still an activity that was widely enjoyed and highly valued: As Mícheál Ó Súilleabháin says:

> *You had this situation of poverty and perhaps because of that there was a lot more leisure time; it's ironic that leisure time can come out of having too much money and can also come out of having not enough. And all we know is that what we call Irish traditional music: the Sean Nós singing, the dance music tradition and the dancing itself is the product of those people.*

THE GREAT FAMINE

> *You'd a population of some eight and a half million people, and between famine, and emigration and ... disease and everything else, it was decimated down to two and a half million. Now in the space of eighty years, if you do that even to a herd of elephants ... you're going to cause havoc ... and the Irish nation, and the Irish people as a whole have a huge psychic hurt which they have pushed way down to the subconscious, but it's still there, and it comes out in various forms.*
>
> PEADAR Ó RIADA[4].

The facts of the Famine are well known in Ireland, but perhaps as Peadar Ó Riada says, the enormity of what happened has been too painful to confront. In 1845 a new strain of blight struck about thirty per cent of the potato crop and destroyed it; in 1846 it destroyed almost all of the crop and for every year after that until the mid-fifties, to a greater or lesser degree, the crop failed. With such a large section of the population totally dependent on the potato, the failure of the crop brought complete devastation. There were scenes of death and disease on a scale never before recorded in Irish

4 Peadar Ó Riada.
Interview, *BIABH*

history. People wandered about the country scavenging for food, dying in the streets, or waiting for death in their cabins. In her autobiography, Peig Sayers, an inhabitant of Great Blasket island off the Kerry coast, recalls her father's account of the Great Famine or 'The Bad Times':

> *'Sixteen years of age I was, Muiris,' he said 'when my uncle died with the hunger ... whatever bit of food was going he preferred to give it to the family so as to keep them alive, but God help us, he failed! The world was too hard ... Hunger got the upper hand of him and he died.'*[5]

Attempts at relief proved inadequate or came too late. Local areas were left to cope with the crisis as best they might. In the west which was worst affected, the fragile structure of public relief collapsed under the strain. Voluntary agencies like the Quakers, money from America, and some landlords stemmed the tide here and there, but these efforts went nowhere near relieving the distress.

Between 1845 and 1855 the face of Ireland was changed for ever. In those ten years one million people died from famine and disease.

Over two million left the country. Those leaving included family groups with young children and infirm elderly people. In the wake of those fleeing the land went artisans and tradesmen whose means of earning a living now had collapsed.

For the first time large numbers left from Irish-speaking areas in the west, which had been very badly hit. In all, perhaps 350 000 Irish speakers emigrated. They were even less well equipped to deal with emigration than their more anglicised compatriots. Handicapped by lack of English they had no cultural resources to deal with the world to which they were going. Their experience of dislocation was intensified on this account.

Those who left and those who died were amongst the most vulnerable – the landless labourers and the smallholders who had no other means of subsistence or way of earning a living outside agriculture.

As if to underline the agony, exports of Irish grain continued uninterrupted throughout the famine years. Nor was this lost on those who survived the famine. A man by the name of Madigan of Kilrush, Co. Clare, composed a song in the 1850s or 1860s which deals with the connected issues of famine and emigration. He does not regard the famine as an 'act of God'.

5 *Peig: The Autobiography of Peig Sayers of the Great Blasket Island*, trans. Bryan MacMahon (Talbot Press, 1974)

The fact was that in addition to British mismanagement, wilful ignorance and callousness, there was a section of Irish Catholic farmers who actually did well out of the famine and used the disaster to rid themselves of unproductive tenants and consolidate their holdings. These tenants were evicted and left to fend for themselves. When Peig's father reminisces about famine times his friend Muiris says: 'Hey, man! ... isn't that how the big farmers came by all the land they have today!'[7]

The Catholic clergy was also responsible for hampering the relief work of Protestant charities. They feared some of their flock might 'turn', i.e. convert to Protestantism, if they accepted the soup being offered by these charities. This was considered to be a greater danger than death from starvation. Even today in Ireland the expression 'to take the soup' carries connotations of sell-out or betrayal.

These subtleties were lost, however, in the upsurge of nationalist feelings in the years after the famine. There was also the guilt that survival imposes on those who make it through a disaster like the famine. This was a phenomenon noted in survivors of Nazi concentration camps. The relief of escape is often accompanied by shame at having done so at the apparent expense of others weaker or more unlucky. It's not surprising then that England became the focus of the anger, and the 'psychic hurt' Peadar Ó Riada speaks of, especially when it could be more than justified on moral grounds. The spirits of the 'coffinless graves of Poor Erin' had to be appeased.

Sad, sad is my fate in this weary exile Dark, dark is the night cloud o'er lone Shanakyle Where the murdered sleep deeply, pile upon pile in the coffinless graves of poor Erin.[6]

THE NEW ISLAND

After-shocks from the famine were felt for many years. Reorganisation of agriculture begun during the famine with the clearance of uneconomic smallholdings continued. Partible inheritance and subdivision of land amongst family members were phased out. Small farms did not disappear though their numbers were reduced. In the west subsistence farming was still carried out. In future family holdings remained intact and were passed on through one heir, usually the eldest son. To facilitate this, emigration was an imperative. Most families could only provide for one son who would inherit the farm. Usually only one daughter could hope for a dowry. Emigration was regarded almost as the duty of the siblings, since remittances from America would help to keep the family farm intact. Nor was there any real incentive

6 'Lone Shanakyle' by
   Madigan, collected by
   Seamus Mac Mathúna,
   from Michael Flanagan
   of Ballyduffbeg, Inagh,
   Co. Clare

7 *Peig*, p. 62

Emigration decimated
the population of places
like the Great Blasket
Island, which was finally
evacuated in 1953. This
article is taken from the
*Springfield Sunday
Republican*,
Massachusetts,
December 1952

NGFIELD, MASS. ● DECEMBER 7, 1952

.AST CHILD
.. doomed Great
.sland is shy little
.eane, whose de-
.or the mainland
.d will leave Blas-
.ut an heir to the
.ons.

NO GIRLS ON BLASKET ISLE

Not a girl remains today on doomed Great Blasket Island, off the coast of Kerry, Ireland, last inhabited island in the most westerly group in Europe. The island is now a puzzled community of 25 — three elderly women, a young wife, a five-year-old boy and a handful of mn. Successive Irish Governments have considered how best to help this dwindling Gaelic colony. They investigated, surveyed, and were torn between a desire to preserve this outpost of an old civilization and at the same time ensure the comfort of the last islanders.
Copyright, Irish News Agency. Distributed by I, N, Photos.

EIGHTY YEARS YOUNG
. . . and brisk as a boy is good-humored Sean O'Sullivan, who built his own house with his hands and the help of his sons.

to migrate within the country, to a town or city. Irish industry collapsed in many towns and cities in the mid-nineteenth century, unable to face competition from cheaper imported goods from Britain and America. Urban workers, clerks, tradesmen, shop assistants and labourers joined the ranks of rural emigrants.

Single women, too, began emigrating in increasing numbers and after 1880 equalled or outstripped the number of males leaving. This was another unique feature of Irish emigration. No other country in the world provided as many unaccompanied single women emigrants as Ireland.

Emigration, while not the desperate flight of famine years, was still viewed as disruptive, painful, dangerous, and involuntary. Many emigration songs attest to this.

Songs of exile and emigration attended the last night of the emigrant. A custom known as the 'American wake' began around the middle of the nineteenth century. Neighbours and family would come to the house for a ritual of farewell which involved music, dancing, drinking and the singing of songs. 'Wakes' often lasted all night and were witnesses to outpourings of grief and emotion. In *Twenty Years A Growing*, Muiris Ó Súilleabháin gives an account of an American wake held for his sister Maura and another girl about to leave Great Blasket Island for Springfield Massachusetts in the 1920s. The passage money was sent to Maura by her aunt in America. She is going because: 'Kate Peg is going and I have no need to stay here when all the girls are departing.'[8] By this time many Blasket islanders had already emigrated. Most of them had relatives in the States. Once the decision to go is made, homesickness and grief sets in.

Maura spends the days before she leaves crying and grieving for the life she will never see again. Of the wake Muiris says,

> *Young and old were gathered in the house, and though music and songs, dancing and mirth, were flying in the air, there was a mournful look on all within. No wonder, for they were all children of the one mother, the people of the Island, no more than twenty yards between any two houses, the boys and girls every moonlight night dancing on the sandhills or sitting together and listening to the sound of the waves from Shingle Strand; and when the moon would wane talking and conversing in the house of old Nell.*[9]

This way of life was based on continuity and tradition and was communal rather than individualistic. In such a context emigration was a huge wrench; it was a kind of death and was mourned as such.

The modern world had not much of a foothold in the life of the Blasket islanders, but their culture was extraordinarily rich. Of the book *Twenty Years A Growing* (originally published in Irish as *Fiche Bliain ag Fás*) and the culture which bore it, the writer E. M. Forster had this to say: '[It is] an account of neolithic civilization from the inside. Synge and others have described it from the outside . . . but I know of no other instance where it has itself become vocal, and addressed modernity.'[10]

While the Blasket community was unique in its state of uninterrupted civilisation there were degrees to which this was true of all of rural Ireland in the nineteenth century. Modernisation was more advanced in some places where, as Irish historian Roy Foster says 'The values of the railway bookstall were replacing those of the street ballad'. But the majority of those emigrating were leaving small farms, and small communally organised societies, where family, kin, and place were the focus of life. Frequently they did not even speak the language of 'An t-Oileán Úr' – the 'New Island' as America was called in Irish. They had no idea what to expect, having no experience of how modern society organised itself.

8 Maurice O'Sullivan, *Twenty Years a Growing* (OUP, 1955), p. 216

9 Ibid., p. 219

10 Ibid., Introduction

Muiris Ó Súilleabháin had this vision of the New Island:

> *It seemed to me that the New Island was before me with its fine streets and great high houses, some of them so tall that they scratched the sky; gold and silver out on the ditches and nothing to do but gather it. I see the boys and girls who were once my companions walking brightly and well contented.*[11]

SONGS OF EXILE AND EMIGRATION

Sarah and Rita Keane of Caherlistrane, Co. Galway, recorded a song for *Bringing It All Back Home*, 'A Stór Mo Chroí', which was often heard at American wakes at the turn of the century. The song is a love song for a child or perhaps a lover on the point of emigrating:

> *A stór mo chroí when you're far away,*
> *from the home you will soon be leaving*
> *tis many a time thro' the night and the day*
> *that your heart it will soon be grieving.*

There is an almost fatalistic acceptance that emigration is inevitable but heart-breaking. The loved one will be in the 'stranger's land' as lonely and sad as the ones left at home. The vista is urban. There is mention of the 'lights of their cities' and the 'throng'. Although there are 'treasures golden' they will not satisfy and the emigrant will pine for the 'long long ago'.

Sara and Rita sing this song in unison in a 'Sean Nós' style, an unusual combination. Unaccompanied, melodic and spare, it avoids sentimentality, while painting a desolate picture of emigration. The air is traditional and predates the lyrics. A version of this song appears in a book published in 1915 entitled *Songs of the Gael*. Its editor, Father Padraig Breathnach was so affected by the lyrics that he expressed the wish that 'it will turn many an intending emigrant from his or her purpose of quitting their native land'.

Another, earlier song which attempts in a very forthright way to do this is 'The Bonny Irish Maid', recorded for *Bringing It All Back Home* by three singers, Phil Callery, Fran McPhail, and Gerry Cullen.

Phil, Fran, and Gerry, all solo singers in their own right, sing

11 Ibid., p. 236

in a choral style not traditional in Irish singing. They use this to great effect on their large repertoire of Irish traditional songs.

The bonny Irish maid of the title attempts to turn her lover's intentions away from emigrating:

Oh many's the foolish youth she said
has gone to some foreign shore
leaving behind his own true love
perhaps to see no more.
It's in crossing of the Atlantic foam
Sometimes their graves are made
Oh stay at home love and do not roam
from your bonny Irish maid.

There are many emigration songs warning of dangers and of intolerable homesickness. One is a song in Irish 'An t-Oileán Úr'. In this account the singer has gone to America on the merest whim, 'A thought came into my head, and I followed it with action, to slip away from my people and go over to America'. He endures the hardships and terrors of the wilds until he meets some Irish people in a backwoods, telling us, interestingly, that he had to speak in English to them. Wonder of wonders, one of them is from his own home place.

The joy of the discovery, however, is quickly replaced by a longing to go home even if it's to die: 'I'd be lucky to be in Ireland even if stretched in a coffin, I'd find "keeners" there to mourn me.'[12]

The bonny Irish maid may have decided to remain at home but thousands of other young Irish women and girls left for America. The Irish nationalist activist and writer Charles J. Kickham commemorated one such woman in a still popular song 'She lives beside the Anner'. Again no good comes of emigration. This 'gentle Irish colleen' has to leave her beautiful (naturally) home place to support her family:

O brave, brave Irish girls!
We well may call you brave –
Sure the least of all your perils
Is the stormy ocean wave.
When you leave your quiet valleys,
And cross the Atlantic foam,
To hoard your hard won earnings
For the helpless ones at home.

(Left to right) Fran McPhail, Phil Callery and Gerry Cullen, 'The Voice Squad', recording 'The Bonny Irish Maid' for *Bringing It All Back Home*

12 Translation by Sean O Boyle, in *The Irish Song Tradition* (Ossian Publications, 1976), p. 79

This brave Irish girls reaches America but dies there, which causes the singer to reflect on 'thy helpless fate, dear Ireland'. In fact most of these women and girls did not die tragic deaths but entered domestic service in the East-Coast cities of America. They had many reasons to do so. Irish society after the famine provided women with three opportunities. Arranged marriage and entering a convent might possibly offer a limited measure of independence. The third option was spinsterhood, spent in domestic service or dependent on ageing parents, and offered none.

In America there was, at least, a measure of personal freedom, financial independence, and the possibility of personal choice in the matter of marriage partner. Not only was this not the case in Ireland, but the opportunities for marrying were very limited. The dowry system, the perpetuation of the family farm and mass emigration had removed those opportunities.

By the 1880s eighty-one per cent of all Irish women immigrants in East-Coast America were in domestic service. Most

The main occupation of Irish women immigrants in America was in domestic service

of them did marry there. A few returned home with their 'dowries' earned, when as it was remarked 'they'd had enough of the washboard'.

They all, men and women, sent millions of dollars home. This money helped support the family, pay rent and ultimately bring brothers and sisters out. The fact that someone had relatives in America was in itself almost a reason for going.

'Ireland's helpless fate' was still uppermost in many emigrants' minds as the cause of emigration. Songs expressing nationalist sentiments were popular and these travelled to America with the emigrants. An incident recounted by John McClancy who kept a diary of his voyage from Queenstown to New York gives a good idea of feelings of the time. He left his home in Co. Clare in 1881 and boarded ship at Queenstown (now Cobh), Co. Cork. Queenstown would have been the most popular port of departure for emigrants in the south of Ireland. There was singing on deck at night amongst the sailors and the passengers, not all of whom were Irish:

> *One Irishman stood up and sang the shamrock so green and the decay of the rose the steward is an English man and when he heard English cut down he rushed and said he would not allow no more of this so the Irish persevered in singing until one Irish man for the good of the Irish to leave [sic] and sing in the bunk so each Irish man descended with black sticks cheering William O'Brien [a nationalist leader] and groaning Balfour [English MP/Chief Secretary for Ireland] we were an over match for the English … so the brave man sang national songs until he made us sleep with them.*[13]

There is no mention in John McClancy's diary of homesickness, but it is evident that the lullabies of the 'brave Irish man' found a welcome response in the hearts of all those Irishmen on board. This identification with Ireland and with the 'cause' of Ireland they kept alive in the New Island.

KILKELLY

Over one hundred and thirty years after his great grandfather left the small village of Kilkelly in Co. Mayo, Peter Jones found a bundle of letters sent to his great grandfather by his father in Ireland. The letters continued from 1860 until the old man's death in 1890. Though not exceptional in any way, they tell

13 Diary of John McClancy of Islandbawn, Miltown Malbay, Co. Clare (Nat. Lib. of Ireland MSS collection, MS 21666)

of family news, births, deaths, sales of land, and bad harvests. They also remind the son that he is still loved, missed and remembered by his family in Ireland. He, in the course of time, marries and has a family in America. One letter tells him that his brother who emigrated to England has returned and is thinking of buying land. The final letter, written by another brother, informs him that his father, whom he has not seen for thirty years, has died. And so the last tangible link with home is broken. Peter Jones used his great great grandfather's letters to make a song which he called 'Kilkelly'. The song was passed on to three Irish musicians living in the USA: Mick Moloney, Jimmy Keane, and Robbie O'Connell are professional musicians who make their living playing music with a strong traditional base. Mick, Jimmy, and Robbie have made 'Kilkelly' their own. It has become emblematic of the kind of immigrant culture they try to bring out in their music. As far as Mick knows it's the only song written 'from the language of emigrant letters, not just in the Irish culture in America but to the best of my knowledge, in any ethnic culture in this country'.

The song has had a deep effect on all audiences. It touches in some fundamental way on the spirit of the emigrant experience. Whenever it is sung people are moved to tears (as witnessed by this writer at a concert in Philadelphia). Mick describes 'Kilkelly' as 'the most eloquent and poignant tale of what it is like to be separated ... the loneliness and the despair of it'.

Throughout the nineteenth century and on into the twentieth century the haemorrhage continued. Between 1856 and 1921, including emigration to Britan, over four million emigrated. From the twenties to the sixties another two million emigrated, mainly to Britain. Most of the emigrants were young men and women, that section of the population with which every healthy country renews itself.

Their going reinforced the conservative social structure that developed after the famine and endured until the mid-1960s; the money they sent home helped sustain poor uneconomic farms, and maintain large families. The writer of the Kilkelly letters makes clear that if it wasn't for American money they would not be able to keep going. Irish-Americans also helped perpetuate emigration not only by paying fares but by finding employment for relatives. Emigration is at the heart of the last two centuries of Irish history and its impact is only beginning to be understood. As Joe Lee has said: 'the imprint left by emigration will feature prominently as the archaeology of the modern Irish mind comes to be excavated.'[14]

14 Joe Lee, *Ireland 1912– 1985* (CUP, 1989)

CHAPTER FOUR

THE WILD ROVERS

The immigrant group which contributed most to American folklore was the Irish.[1]

One way in which the movement of the Irish through America can be traced is through song. Many traditional songs, like 'Rose Connolly', travelled with the immigrants, and while some endured unaltered, many were adapted. Around their experiences a new repertoire emerged: railroad songs, lumberjack songs, work songs, songs of love and adventure, of exploitation, comic songs, nostalgic songs and songs of home. Many of these songs passed out of the preserve of the purely ethnic group and entered the mainstream of American folk song. Just as the music of the Appalachian Scots-Irish was assimilated into the wider folk culture a century earlier, the music of mid-nineteenth-century Irish emigrants met and mingled with the music of other peoples.

The two musical streams met on the railroads, in construction camps, and farms, in travelling shows and in the music halls.

One of the most fruitful encounters in the history of modern folk song is that which occurred between the Irish and Afro-American music cultures.

1 A Green, *Railroad Songs
and Ballads from the
Archive of Folk Culture*
(Lib. of Congress,
Washington)

THE WORKING LIFE

The years immediately following the Great Famine were difficult for Irish emigrants to the east coast of America. They had endured famine at home; dangerous and pestilential sea voyages had killed thousands of them, and many were so broken in health and mind that they were unfit for work.

What work they could get was menial, hard and poorly paid. They worked in building construction, docking, machine shops, mines, and on canal and railroad construction. They lived in slum conditions in all the cities they settled in and their mortality from disease was high.

POOR PADDY WORKS ON THE RAILWAY

In eighteen hundred and forty one
I put me cordroy britches on.
I put me cordroy britches on
To work upon the railway, the railway,
I'm weary of the railway,
Poor Paddy works on the railway.

This song is one of the earliest recorded railroad songs and predates the famine exodus. It was already a popular song by the time the first track of the transcontinental railroad was laid in 1863 when the Union Pacific railway company laid tracks westward from Omaha. At the same time the Central Pacific began moving eastward from Sacramento.

Thousands of Irish workers, many of them ex-soldiers who had fought in the American Civil War, worked on this epic construction. They travelled with the section gangs living in work camps struck by the company along the route. Railroads and railroad construction spawned a new lore of songs, stories and tunes which in time became a definitive part of American folk culture. From 'The Wreck of the Old Ninety-Seven' to the 'Chatanooga Choo Choo' the train is an evocative symbol of 'conquest, escape, resignation, love and death'. In the songs of the railroad Americans recognise themselves and their nation's history and folk lore.

There are the work songs sung by the black section gangs to the rhythm of timber-felling, track-laying, hammering and spike-driving. There are songs of exploitation, songs of adventure and of travelling, of outlaws and of hoboes. The image of the hobo riding the freight train is one which still appears in contemporary American popular song.

On the transcontinental line there were section gangs composed entirely of Irishmen. There were even section gangs which were made up of only Irish-speaking Irishmen.

I landed in this country
a year and a month ago.
To make my living at labouring work
to the railroad I did go.

The hero of this song, Mike Cahooley, is an exemplary railroad worker. He works so hard that he is made the boss of the section gang in a year:

I'm the walking boss of the whole railroad
for none I care a dang,
My name is Mike Cahooley
And I'm the boss of the section gang.

Promontory, Utah. This is where the transcontinental railroad was completed in 1869. Thousands of Irishmen worked on its construction. Pay was $3 a day

Mike Cahooley was typical of many of the Irish working on the transcontinental line. The work was hard; the pay was three dollars a day and the Irish were well regarded as workers. There were competitions between the eastward and westward workers to see who could lay the most track in a day and this speeded up construction. On average they laid three miles a day and each line employed between 8000 and 10 000 workers.

The Irish worked mainly on the Central Pacific, and their work camps along the route grew into the towns and cities of the Midwest.

The two lines met at Promontory Utah on 10 May 1869, six years after work began. Within twenty years the last of the major railway construction would be finished and the frontier would no longer exist. Of this generation of Irish and Irish-Americans the great song collector Alan Lomax says:

Damn be the President My name is Mike. I got a hand in it, I drive the spike.[2]

> **They brought little besides their strength, their wit, and their singing tradition with them, but without them America, and especially the railroads of America would never have been built....**
>
> **These lads were the principal singers in the lumber camps and on the canals. We know that they sang as they built the Erie, the Pennsylvania, and the Union Pacific.**

THE HILLS OF GLENSHEE: MUSIC OF THE LUMBERJACK

Pete Seeger, whose beanpole frame is usually associated with the five-string banjo, has an Irish tune in his repertoire which he likes to play on the recorder. It's called 'The Hills of Glenshee'. Pete learned the air from an old lumberjack in the Catskill Mountains many years ago. It was, he says, originally a love song but the words got lost along the way. The air had come to the lumberjack through his mother. Perhaps it originally had Irish words and so fell out of use with the adoption of English by Irish-speaking immigrants.

In the lumber camps, according to the collector Helene Stratman-Thomas, 'the English speaking Irish seem to have been the principal bards.' Certainly there are plenty of examples of songs of Irish derivation emanating from this source. An outlaw song for example, 'Brennan on the Moor', still very popular in Ireland, has been collected in the lumber camps and in other parts of America. An American Library

2 John and Alan Lomax, *Best Loved American Folk Songs* (Grosset and Dunlop, 1947)

of Congress collection made in the lumber camp regions of Wisconsin includes a very interesting song with the title 'I'll Sell my Hat, I'll Sell my Coat'. In Ireland this song is known by the Irish title, 'Siúil a Rún', and was recorded as recently as the mid-seventies by Clannad, a band from Donegal who reworked many old traditional songs in an idiom incorporating folk, jazz and rock.

The song dates from the seventeenth century and is living proof that a good folk song never dies.

'Siúil a Rún' is one of a very small number of traditional songs known as 'macaronic'. These macaronic songs include lines in both the Irish and English language, and date from a time and place when the spoken language of the people was in transition from Irish to English. Sometimes the lines are alternately Irish and English, but here the chorus is in Irish and the verses in English. In the American version, the man promises to sell his hat and coat to 'buy my wife a little flat boat'. The Irish version has the girl promise to sell her spinning-wheel to buy her love 'a sword of steel'.

To overcome the problem of the Irish-language chorus, the American version substitutes a nonsense-word rigmarole to approximate the sound of the Irish words. The first line of the chorus in Irish is 'Siúil, siúil, siúil, a rún' (Walk, walk, walk my love)'. In the American version this becomes 'Shule, shule, shule – i rue', continuing in this vein, fitting the nonsense words to the metre of the Irish chorus.

YOU'RE WELCOME HERE KIND STRANGER

In 1946 Helene Stratman-Thomas recorded a Mrs Frances Perry of Black River Falls in Wisconsin singing 'The Lakes of Ponchartrain'. Mrs Stratman-Thomas noted that Mrs Perry learned the song from a family of settlers from Georgia. She also remarked that the song was to be found all over America 'from Nova Scotia to Texas'.

The hero, a weary traveller in the southern states falls in love with a beautiful Creole girl whom he meets on the lakes of Ponchartrain. She offers him the hospitality of her parents' house:

You're welcome here kind stranger
our house is very plain
But we never turn a stranger out
On the Lakes of Ponchartrain.

In Ireland the song was recorded nearly twenty years ago by Christy Moore, one of the country's most popular singers of ballads. He learned the song from the English traditional singer, Martin Carthy. In 1978 another Irish singer then singing folk and traditional material, Paul Brady, recorded the song for his first solo album, which took its title, 'Welcome Here Kind Stranger' from a line in the song. It is supposed in Ireland that the young man is a soldier returning home from the American Civil War. Over 200 000 Irishmen did fight in the American Civil War, although mostly on the Union side.

Whatever the young man's identity, the song has a beautiful melancholy air which recently claimed another Irish singer, Liam Ó Maonlaí. Liam is a young singer and musician, whose band The Hothouse Flowers reflects his eclectic musical tastes from 'Sean Nós' singing in Irish (Liam is a fluent Irish speaker) to blues and rock. 'I'm trained through Sean Nós,' says Liam, 'but that lends itself to an awful lot of modern rock, soul, blues singing ... and lends itself to my own style of singing'.

Liam Ó'Maonlaí (at the piano) of Hothouse Flowers, with Leo Barnes at a *Bringing It All Back Home* recording session

Certainly something at the heart of 'The Lakes of Pon-chartrain' caught Liam; 'Paul Brady I heard singing that song ... and I just fell in love with it ... and we just had to do it.' Liam and the band recorded a fine version of the song for *Bringing It All Back Home*, Liam singing and accompanying himself at the piano with Leo Barnes providing a rich and evocative sax solo.

NO IRISH NEED APPLY

> *[The Irish] were the first major European unskilled
> ethnic group to come and settle in this land ... a new
> land where they found that the old masters were still in
> the ascendancy. A lot of discrimination ensued and songs
> that mirror that abound ... songs which show how the
> Irish were discriminated against and how negative
> stereotypes of the Irish abounded.*
>
> MICK MOLONEY[3]

> *[The Irish] were the first group, except native Americans
> and blacks, about whom there grew unflattering,
> mordant, and hostile stereotypes.*
>
> JOHN AND SELMA APPEL[4]

The arrival of large groups of unskilled, poor, famished, and sometimes diseased Irish to the cities and towns of East-Coast America horrified the incumbent Protestant establishment. The Irish suffered extreme dislocation. The majority were from rural backgrounds unfamiliar with city life. The work practices and ethics of an industrialised society were alien to them, and a sizeable proportion had no English. Their world view was pre-modern; their customs and social patterns were communalistic, non-literate, and traditional.

The adjustment was painful and took several years. In the meantime they were met with hostility, suspicion, bigotry and racism. Their arrival had coincided with the age of industrial expansion in America. They were the first emigrant group to provide the muscle and brawn that this demanded. Their first experience of work was of exploitation and discrimination.

In the coalmines they were paid low wages and were compulsorily bound to the company store and housing. Frequently they were hired for wages which were halved when too many turned up for the jobs. One Irish emigrant described the life of an Irish labourer in America as: 'despicable, humiliating and slavish ... [There] was no love for him – no protection of life, [he] can be shot down, run through, kicked, cuffed, spat on – and no redress, but a response of served the damn son of an Irish b—— right, damn him.'[5] Everywhere the Irish settled, 'No Irish Need Apply' notices followed them.

3 Mick Moloney. Interview, *BIABH*

4 John and Selma Appel, *Pat-riots to Patriots, American Irish in Caricature and Comic Art* (Michigan State University Museum, 1990)

5 Kerby Miller, *Emigrants and Exiles – Ireland and the Irish Exodus to North America* (OUP, 1985), p. 323

Researching in the American Library of Congress in the late forties, Pete Seeger came across two almost identical song texts on the subject of discrimination, dating from this period in Irish-American history. He put them together and made the song he has been singing ever since 'No Irish Need Apply'. The Irishman in this song has to adopt the role assigned to him by the caricaturists in the absence of any other alternative. He opts for confronting the employer who has posted a 'No Irish Need Apply' notice.

Well I couldn't stand his nonsense
So a hoult of him I took,
And I gave him such a batin'
As he'd get in Donnybrook
And he hollered meela murder
And to get away did try
And he swore he'd never write again
No Irish need apply.

This stratagem as a way of making bigots see sense leaves something to be desired and it was to take a generation or two before other less violent means could dismantle the apparatus of discrimination.

Labour unions were suppressed and many Irish workers got involved in secret societies. Many of them were familiar with this form of organisation in Ireland. One of the most famous secret organisations was the Molly Maguires set up in the anthracite fields of Pennsylvania in the 1860s. The anthracite miners were forced to work under abominable conditions and were prevented from striking or negotiating with their bosses. They retaliated by forming the Molly Maguires. This organisation was responsible for the murders of mine managers and informers. They were eventually caught and nineteen of them hanged.

By the 1880s labour organisations were in a strong enough position to establish the American Federation of Labour. By the turn of the century the AFL represented seventy-five per cent of all organised labour in the US. The Irish predominated in the early labour unions. Irish women were notably active. The famous 'Mother Jones' who organised for the miners' union was Mary Harris of County Cork. Lenora O' Reilly organised the garment workers of New York, and Elizabeth Gurley Flynn became one of the most radical and able labour organisers of the twentieth century.

CARTOON PADDY

The social lives of the Irish repelled the city elders; their tendency to cling together in ghettos gave them the name 'Shanty Irish'. Their drinking, riotous wakes, dances and quarrelling brought down the wrath of the policeman and the magistrate. Out of their lives and occupations came the 'Paddy' and 'Biddy' stereotypes which dogged them for decades.

The Irishman with his clay pipe in his gob was depicted as an ape-man. Portrayed in a variety of guises designed to demonstrate his stupidity, barbarity, drunkenness, shiftlessness and lawlessness, 'Pat' was a stock cartoon character.

A cartoon entitled 'Uncle Sam's Lodging House' (above) depicts amongst all the other well-behaved representatives of America's immigrant nations one brawling Irish ape-man in his bunk. He is waving a bottle of whiskey and 'giving the finger' to his host, Uncle Sam. This cartoon appeared in *Puck*, a popular weekly magazine, in June 1892. Underneath, the editorial reads 'The raw Irishman in America is a nuisance, his son a curse. They never assimilate; the second generation shows an intensification of all the bad qualities of the first ... they are a burden and a misery to this country.'

This attitude prevailed until the turn of the century. By then the stereotype had evolved into a lovable rogue with the gift of the gab. Paddy became a feckless, charming and amusing fellow, harmless, and not to be taken seriously. Those Irish who had by now managed to climb up a rung or two on the ladder were characterised as 'lace curtain Irish' and their petit-bourgeois pretensions were ridiculed. From the 1850s onwards weekly magazines like *Puck* and the new newspaper comic strips developed their stock of Irish stereotypes. The ape-man gave way to the cop, the hod-carrier, the washer-woman, the colleen, the saloon-keeper, the ward politician, and the Irish drunk. The latter is identified as an Irish character to this day.

SHAMROCKS, SHILLELAGHS AND SHENANNIGANS

Irish Americans, particularly the second generation Irish, participated eagerly in the new American mass culture. It was a Casey after all who was at bat, a Sullivan and a Corbett in the ring, and Harrigans, Harts, Rooneys and Cohans romping on vaudeville stages.

TIMOTHY J. MEAGHER[6]

The variety stage and vaudeville, burlesque and slapstick – this was the popular entertainment of immigrants in nineteenth-century American cities.

From the 1850s, in every city, there were music halls offering several different shows.

Music-hall audiences were characterised by their lack of restraint and their involvement with the show. They sang along, they ate, laughed and roared at the performers whom they knew by name. Stock Irish characters took to the music-hall stage early on. They were never objects of racist ridicule. In a way the music hall and vaudeville show gave back to immigrants what the crude caricatures of comic strips and cartoons took away.

Stage Irishmen like 'Throw him Down Mc Closkey' and 'Mc Ginty' landed in all sorts of scrapes but came through, often at the expense of the uppity Yankee.

Music hall belonged to immigrants. On the music-hall stage they heard their own accents, saw their own world, their own hopes and dreams of America.

Edward Harrigan was an acclaimed writer for the variety stage. With his song writer Dave Braham, and actor Tony Hart he enjoyed decades of uninterrupted popularity. Harrigan was the grandson of Irish emigrants and had grown up in an Irish slum in Manhattan. At this time in the 1860s there was more Irish spoken there than English. Twenty-six per cent of the population of New York when he was a boy, about 133 000

6 Timothy J. Meagher, 'From Paddy to Studs', *Irish American Communities 1880–1920* (Greenwood Press, 1986)

people, were Irish born. About one third of them would have been Irish speakers.

From the 1870s to the end of the century he produced plays for the variety stage. They featured the beggars, maids, street-sellers, landlords, hod-carriers, Germans, Jews, and Irish of the city of immigrants. 'I have sought above all,' he said, 'to make all my plays like pages from actual life.'

There was a strong Irish element to the songs in Harrigan shows. A song from a Harrigan and Hart show, *The Merry Malones* called 'Danny by my Side' was a favourite of the Irish-American Governor of New York, Alfred E. Smith. He sang the song at a ceremony to celebrate the fiftieth anniversary of the completion of the Brooklyn Bridge. The bridge owed more than a little to the labour of Irish workers, many of whom had died on its construction.

Irish music was also assimilated into variety. An early encounter was with the music of black America. The outcome was evident in the first dance routines of the early variety-show entertainers. Thomas Dartmouth 'Daddy' Rice is credited with marrying an Irish fiddle tune to an Afro-American shuffle dance thereby 'inventing' the 'soft shoe shuffle' routine which became the popular minstrel dance 'Jump Jim Crow'. An Irishman by the name of Dan Emmet was one of the first blackface minstrels and wrote 'Dixie' and the 'Blue Tail Fly'. This was another staple minstrel routine, and was a mixture of Irish hornpipe and a black tune 'Jim Crack Corn'. Out of all these routines evolved the 'buck and wing' and 'soft shoe shuffle', steps which became basic to all song and dance acts.

These pioneers of variety would have agreed with Edward Harrigan when he said that he returned to the themes of runaway slaves and Irish immigrants because the Irish and the blacks were the two races who cared most about song and dance.

As a young man Jerry Cohan made several appearances in Harrigan and Hart shows. He was the son of Famine-Irish immigrants and was an acclaimed traditional dancer. The act he developed featured updated versions of jigs and reels. In time he went on the road with a show called the *Hibernicon*, a rag-bag of sketches, comic acts, and song and dance routines. He also toured with his wife and two children as 'The Four Cohans'. His son George M. Cohan was to become an American archetype – the Song and Dance Man. In Cohan's hands, music hall severed its links with immigrant culture and became American.

The two big strains in American music are Ireland and Africa.
PETE SEEGER[7]

7 Pete Seeger. Interview, *BIABH*

YANKEE DOODLE DANDY

I'm a Yankee Doodle Dandy Yankee Doodle, do or die A real live nephew of my Uncle Sam Born on the fourth of July.

'Yankee Doodle Dandy' appears in a show, *Little Johnny Jones*, of 1904. This song and 'Give my Regards to Broadway' were the two smash hits of the year. The show was written, directed and produced by George M. Cohan who also played the lead.

He claimed to have been born on 4 July, although his birth certificate says 3 July. He was in all other respects a Yankee Doodle Boy, the grandson of Irish immigrants fleeing the Famine. In two generations he came to embody an essentially American spirit, plucky, enterprising and patriotic. The Catholic church in America had realised early on that the way to full acceptance lay in patriotic allegiance to the flag, even if some cultural baggage had to be shed along the way. They had used the pulpit and schools to get the point across and had been more or less successful.

George, in his show, *George Washington Junior* produced another hit on this very theme, 'You're a Grand Old Flag'. His shows sold out and succeeded in spite of the attacks of critics in the 'quality papers'. He was criticised for being 'vulgar cheap and blatant'. Bob Callahan describes him as 'nothing more or less than the very spirit of turn-of-the-century America itself, with the throttle pushed all the way to the floor....'[8]

George M. Cohan's contribution was significant in purely musical terms. His dance routines, songs, even his way of holding his body on stage were all copied. His 'Give My Regards to Broadway' and 'Yankee Doodle Dandy' became American anthems.

In 'Thousands are Sailing' Philip Chevron celebrates Cohan's contribution to American popular culture:

And we said goodnight to Broadway giving it our best regards tipped our hats to Mr Cohan dear old Time Square's favourite bard.

WHEN IRISH EYES ARE SMILING

The musicians and their music performed on the music-hall stage in the nineteenth century entertained an immigrant audience with the stuff of their own lives. Irish material was worked into the plots and songs and dialogue in a way that reflected the new reality of immigrant life. By the end of the century

8 Bob Callahan, *The Big Book of American-Irish Culture* (Viking, 1987), p. 14

some of these stage Irishisms were already a throwback. They embarrassed the Irish on their way out to the suburbs. Audiences were no longer eating and drinking in the stalls and roaring disapproval or approval to the players on the stage. Not many Irish-Americans wanted to be reminded of the reality of tenement life as they were about to take their first step out of it. Like James Tyrone in Eugene O'Neill's play *Long Day's Journey into Night* they had long memories. They knew 'the value of a dollar and the fear of the poorhouse'.

They wanted to forget the bad times and remember what good times there were. If none could be found they could be invented. Tin Pan Alley (the collective name for the music publishing business based around New York's 28th Street) was happy to oblige. Its songsmiths produced thousands of 'Oirish' numbers from the quaint to the downright sentimental. From this source came a song which entered the repertoire of every Irish tenor, 'Mother Machree' written by one of Tin Pan Alley's principal balladeers, Chauncey Olcott. He also wrote what Mick Moloney describes as 'the anthem of mainstream Irish America' – 'When Irish Eyes are Smiling':

When Irish hearts are happy
All the world seems bright and gay,
And when Irish eyes are smiling
Sure they steal your heart away.

'Mother Machree' was the stage favourite of the internationally acclaimed Irish tenor John McCormack who toured America in the teens and twenties.

McCormack himself was at the centre of an incident which betrayed an ambivalence at the core of Irish-American self-perception. The renowned Irish piper Patsy Touhey travelled the States on the variety circuit in stage shows like the Cohans' *Hibernicon*. As well as playing the uilleann pipes he performed a Mick and Pat routine. This was a comic act of the stage-Irish sort. He and McCormack were on the same bill at the New Orleans Fair in 1911. McCormack was so incensed by Touhey's display of paddywhackery that he demanded that the act be taken out of the set. Eventually clownish Paddy the Irishman disappeared altogether. Other characters waited in the wings . . . smiling cops, priests with hearts of gold, and colleens. Their American allegiance was in no doubt.

Irish immigrants who came to America in the late nineteenth and early twentieth century were better equipped to cope with

Piper Patrick Touhey was
one of the first Irish
traditional musicians to
be commercially recorded
in America

the life that lay ahead of them. They were better educated
than their illiterate and famished forebears. They were linked
into an established Irish-American network of relations and
neighbours. Through these connections they could get jobs and
accommodation. They were well set up to assimilate. There
were others who came with no English and from backgrounds
thousands of cultural years away from American life. There
were always those who never wavered in their allegiance to
Ireland and all that that entailed culturally and politically.
Nationalism of every hue from radical revolutionary to con-
stitutionalist found a home in Irish America and still does.

Irish historian Roy Foster says that Ireland: 'claimed a
fiercely and unrealistically obsessive identification from its
emigrants'. It must be said that this 'obsessive identification'
ensured that a musical tradition long in the doldrums in Ireland
would stay alive in America and live to go back home.

CHAPTER FIVE

THE JIG OF LIFE

We sit up there on the stage and play concerts ... but people will invariably say at the end of the night: 'God, we were dying to get up and dance'.[1]

FRANKIE GAVIN OF DE DANANN

The instrumental traditional music of Ireland is mainly dance music and mostly dates from the eighteenth century.

At the outset it was part of a rich and active tradition of dancing that reached its peak of popularity towards the end of the eighteenth century and maintained it for nearly a century. This despite the devastation of the Great Famine and the disapproval of the Catholic church.

Although a great player was always listened to, the primary function of a musician was to provide music for dancing.

In the nineteenth century Irish traditional music first began to separate from the dance, as we shall see. This important development shaped the future of traditional music in America and in Ireland.

THE IRISH TRADITION OF DANCE

Accounts of life in seventeenth- and early eighteenth-century Ireland attest to dancing as a popular activity. Round or group dances where the dancers formed a long line or a circle seem to have been in vogue, but we have very

1 Frankie Gavin.

Interview, *BIABH*

little idea of what these dances looked like or how the music sounded. The two words in Irish which mean dance, 'damhsa' and 'rince', are both borrowed from English. Jigs and reels, the two main dances, derive from Italian and Anglo-Saxon respectively.

At the heart of the eighteenth- and nineteenth-century dancing tradition was the travelling dancing master who spent six weeks or so in a parish and then moved on.

Crossroads' dances were a feature of social life in rural Ireland well into the twentieth century

As Mícheál Ó Súilleabháin has pointed out, the life of the mainly peasant population was subsistence farming which left plenty of time with nothing to do. This enforced leisure was partly filled with music and dancing. The arrival of the itinerant dancing master was eagerly anticipated because it meant a period of more or less continuous dancing and one or two 'big nights' with entertainment and drink.

The eighteenth-century traveller in Ireland Arthur Young noted: 'Dancing ... is almost universal in every cabbin. Dancing masters ... travel through the country from cabbin to cabbin with a piper or blind fiddler; and the pay is sixpence a quarter. It is an absolute system of education'.

Each dancing master had his own collection of parishes and townlands which he visited, and the dancing masters respected each other's territory. Occasionally there might be a competition between two masters to see who would 'get' a particular parish. The dancing master would put up in the house of a local farmer or spend a night in turn with each of his pupils. He took his pupils as he found them, the usual mixed bag of the naturally gifted and the 'two left feet variety' of dancer.

The basic steps taught to the dancers were the jig and reel. Within each dance, stamping, shuffling, grinding, and skipping and hopping steps were danced.

A feature of Irish dancing which has remained the same to this day is the particular stance of the dancer. There is no movement of the body above the hips. Relatively little floor space is covered by the dancer or dancers. The solo dancer often danced on a single plank of wood or a door taken off its hinges for the purpose. As Breandán Breathnach says, 'The good dancer danced, as it were underneath himself trapping each note of the music on the floor.'[2]

A good dancer would be taught pieces for solo performance incorporating these steps, and also special exhibition dances known as set dances. These talented pupils probably went on to become dancing masters themselves. The other pupils were taught round or group dances, because dancing had a social function and was a popular pastime at weddings, festivals and so on. Dancing was completely interwoven into the fabric of community life. It came as naturally as talking, story-telling, or singing, and remained a feature of rural life for over three hundred years.

In his diary of his voyage on an emigrant ship from Queenstown, Co. Cork to New York in 1881, John J. McClancy mentions the favoured ways of passing time on board.

'About eve ... we had music and dance of all kinds we had great fun in the Germans the way they dance is wheeling around always like we would dance a polka.' And 'When we come up in the morning we dont go down until night the boys and girls are to and fro over the deck we have great games dancing and singing.'

Again: 'Wednesday morning there was heavy rain and fog thunder and lightening we remained down dancing for most part of the day.'[3]

> *I like playing for dancing, it makes sense for me; I don't see much point in playing music unless there's somebody dancing to it.*
> SEAMUS BEGLEY, WEST KERRY MUSICIAN

2 Breandán Breathnach, *Folk Music and Dances of Ireland*, p. 53

3 Diary of John McClancy

THE MUSIC OF THE DANCE

> *Irish music is not merely not European, it is quite remote from it. It is, indeed, closer to some forms of oriental music. The first thing we must do, if we are to understand it, is to forget about European music. Its standards are not Irish standards; its style is not Irish style; its forms are not Irish forms.*[4]
>
> SEÁN Ó RIADA[4]

'Then a fig for the new fashioned waltzes imported from Spain and from France, and a fig for the thing called the polka, our own Irish jig will we dance.' From a postcard published by Lawrence of Dublin

The first thing that must be said about Irish traditional music is that it does not use the same scales as European or Western music of the last two centuries. These are the major and minor scales on which all Western music is based. A scale is a collection of notes with set intervals of tones or half tones between the notes. In Western music the scale is a seven-gapped scale of eight notes, called an octave. In tonic solfa these notes are known as Doh, Ray, Mi, Fah, Soh, La, Ti, Doh. The tonic or bottom note normally gives the scale its key, and the notes of the scale will have the same relationship to each other regardless of key. The minor scale differs from the major in one respect. The interval between the second and third note is a half tone, as opposed to a full-tone interval in the major.

Irish music on the other hand is modal. In the modal system it is possible to have seven scales and Irish music uses four of these. All this means is that there is a different and more interesting tonal character to traditional music. There are possibilities which do not apply in Western music. The traditional music of England and America is also modal.

Western ears are more attuned to harmonic music where notes are sounded together as in chords or harmony singing. Irish music is essentially monophonic (single sound) and depends on a single decorated melody line.

Endings are not as found in Western art music, where there is theme, variation and resolution. In traditional music, particularly the dance music, the tune can be repeated as often as desired, and the last phrase of one tune leads naturally to the beginning of another.

As demonstrated in Chapter 1, whistle player Mary Bergin playing 'The Blackberry Blossom' reel moves without stopping into a second reel 'Lucky In Love', using the final note of the first as a bridge. And Paddy Glackin, Ricky Skaggs, and Mark O'Connor, who recorded the same reel for *Bringing It All Back Home*, also use this technique but play 'The Saint Anne's Reel'.

4 Seán Ó Riada, *Our Musical Heritage*, p. 20

There are no rules about what goes with what. The music stopping is dictated by the wish of the musicians to move on to something else, or by the structure of the dance.

The music is not developed, resolved and brought to a conclusion in the classical sense. The Irish composer Seán Ó Riada described the circular nature of Irish music as:

> *the graph of real life. Every day the sun rises, every day it sets. Every day possesses the same basic characteristics, follows the same fundamental pattern, while at the same time each day differs from the last in its ornamentation of events.*[5]

So with circularity goes ornamentation. Without it the music would be boring and monotonous, the same each time it is played. Ornamentation makes it possible for a tune to be different, each time it is played. It is still the same tune, as a day is still a day, and is different in the way that one day is from another.

Ornamentation offers three possibilities. One is to decorate the tune by adding trills, triplets, or grace notes. The second is to change the order of the melody but not so much that the tune is bent out of shape. The third is to make slight variations in the rhythm or metre of the piece. There is a vocabulary which musicians use to describe these effects: cranning, rolling, double-stopping, are some of the terms. So learning the melody line is only the beginning of learning how to play traditional music.

Some musicians like to use other musicians' 'settings' of tunes rather than attempt to do them themselves. This also demands a lot of the player, bearing in mind that any one player may have over two hundred tunes in his or her repertoire. It is also easy to see how what in Western music would be a very short melody is laden with infinite possibilities. Listen to fiddler Paddy Glackin describe a reel which he recorded with his brothers Seamus and Kevin for *Bringing It All Back Home*:

> *'The Glen Road to Carrick' – that's a timeless tune; that's a tune one would never get fed up of for the simple reason it's such an interesting tune; there are five parts in it and there are so many possibilities within that that makes it so interesting.*

5 Ibid., p. 21

A musician's ability to ornament a tune is very highly regarded and, as Seán Ó Riada said, this kind of musician is 'a creative contributor to the tradition. He makes it grow and develop.' Irish music, then, is circular, melodic and ornamented. It makes little use of dynamics – there is no loud and soft, little vibrato. The musical quality arises from the melody, the ornamentation of the melody and the instrument used.

Irish music is, as I have said, orally transmitted. In the days before recorded music, motor cars and mass communications, a traditional musician learned tunes locally. Each region had its own particular style of playing, its own particular tunes. Sometimes a preference for a particular instrument developed, like fiddles or flutes in Sligo, or concertinas in Clare. There are few players left in Ireland who are exclusively regional in their playing. Brothers John and Paddy Killourhy are. They learned their music from neighbours in their part of West Clare, a county famous for traditional music and players. Their repertoire and style is uninfluenced by players from other parts of Ireland or by radio or records. They have never moved out of their own locality and as John says: 'we've played for country dances all our lives'. For them there is no separation of playing from dancing.

Brothers Paddy and John Killourhy in their home in Co. Clare. All their lives they have played traditional music for house dances

THE DANCES

The most popular dances are jigs and reels and they constitute the majority of tunes.

JIGS

Jigs, according to Breandán Breathnach, are the oldest dance tunes in Ireland today. Jigs come in three forms: single jigs, double jigs, and slip jigs, depending on the arrangement of notes within the bar.

REELS

The reel is by far the most popular playing tune because of its fast fluid rhythm. It's also common to the whole country. Reels are played in 4/4 time with two groups of four quavers to the bar. Many reel tunes are Scottish in origin. The popular reel 'Miss Mc Leods' for example is common to the Scots, Irish and American tradition.

HORNPIPES

The hornpipe dance is of English origin. Hornpipes are in 4/4 time like the reels, played slower, and more heavily accented. Hornpipes are not so plentiful as jigs and reels but they are in every player's repertoire.

SLIDES AND POLKAS

Until recently slides and polkas were mainly heard in the south and west of the country in Clare, Cork, Limerick and Kerry, and were especially associated with one particular area of the country, Sliabh Luachra, on the Cork Kerry border. Slides and polkas are popular with musicians from this area, and musicians interested in this style of playing. With these exceptions, they are not as frequently heard as reels and jigs. The polka is in 2/4 time and the slide in 6/8.

HIGHLANDS

Highlands are associated with the regional playing of Donegal in the far north-west of the country. This county had a lot of contact, through seasonal migration, with neighbouring Scotland, and music came back along this route. The highland is known in Scotland as the highland fling and is a national dance. In Donegal the tunes were adapted and enjoyed great popularity with fiddle players.

Frankie Gavin and
Yehudi Menuhin
recording an Irish
hornpipe in New York for
*Bringing It All Back
Home*

As Mairéad Ní Mhaonaigh, fiddle player from Donegal, describes them, the highlands are 'slower reels; they're still in 4/4 time like a reel would be but . . . slower . . . the rhythm is more measured'.

Dance music is played as instrumental music nowadays. But dancing still goes on, and indeed the country is in the midst of a major revival of set dancing at the moment. Reels, jigs, and hornpipes are all in the repertoire of solo dancers, but also make up the group or 'set' dancing routines. Slides and polkas on the other hand are only played for set dancing where two or four pairs of dancers dance together.

THE CHURCH AND DANCING

Dancing is . . . a thing which leads . . . to bad thoughts and evil actions . . . it is dancing that excites the desires of the body. . . . In the dance are seen frenzy and woe, and with dancing thousands go to the black hell.

DONAL O'COLMAIN, PARISH PRIEST, 1670[6]

6 Parliament na Mban
(Ed Brian O Cuiv, Dublin,
1952) Trans Breandán
Breathnach

For nearly three hundred years the Catholic church in Ireland inveighed against their parishioners' main pastime – dancing. From the seventeenth century onwards the Catholic clergy in many parts of the country actively waged campaigns against dancing. They had considerable power at their disposal, the ultimate penalty invoked being excommunication. Their opposition to what was nothing more than a harmless and enjoyable country pleasure was groundless. The stated reasons were, as outlined above, moral ones. Dancing was sinful because it led to sins of promiscuity and drunkenness. Girls lost their virtue and boys became libertines and drunks. 'Pattern' or 'Patron' days in particular came in for strong clerical censure. These were originally the feast days of a local saint or patron and were held at some holy spot like a well associated with the saint. After a certain amount of praying and penance the assembly got down to celebrating the day with music, dancing, and drinking. According to Sir Henry Piers who observed a pattern day in 1682, 'the day is spent as if they celebrated the Bacchanalia, rather than the memory of a pious saint'. Sir Henry found the dancing 'lewd and obscene'. One hundred years later, another traveller in Ireland, John Carr, found the Sunday practice of dancing entirely charming, 'a spirit of gaiety shines upon every hour, the bagpipe is heard, and every foot is in motion'. The bishop of Cashel and Emly in 1796 threatened that if any behaviour other than strict religious devotions was observed on the patron day in his diocese the feast day would be suppressed. Those who had transgressed by singing, dancing, or merry-making would be excommunicated.

There is little evidence to connect dancing with debauchery, although pattern days did frequently get out of hand. As Breandán Breathnach pointed out in his article 'The Church and Dancing In Ireland',[8] most of the dancing was solo dancing and, where there were group dancers, the boys and girls did not hold one another. Captain Francis O'Neill, the great collector of Irish music in America, remained bitter to the end of his days about the way the clergy had 'capriciously and arbitrarily' suppressed the music in his home place near Bantry in west Cork. He considered their opposition 'senseless hostility' since all dances were held in public, often in the open air, and always 'among friends and neighbours'.

Whatever the reasons, clerical opposition and interference continued right up to the middle of this century. Stories about priests breaking up house parties, barn dances, open-air dancing, beating up musicians, and breaking instruments abound. In Captain O'Neill's parish of Caherea in west Cork the local piper, who was blind and made his living from piping, was forced into the poorhouse in Bantry after the parish priest banned crossroads and house dances. This took place around 1860 and may have been one of the reasons that young Francis O'Neill, a brilliant musician, took off for America at the age of sixteen in 1864. There was no more music at home.

I'll tell you what killed them [the house dances] too, will I? The clergy killed them, the priests. There was crying out of the pulpits that the divil was inside in the house, the divil for the dance. They caused terrible trouble. They put all the youth of the country into the dance halls that was in the towns; they stopped the country dances.
JOHN KILLOURHY[7]

7 John Killourhy.
   Interview, *BIABH*

8 Breandán Breathnach,
   Dal gCais, 1982

There is a terrible account of an incident which took place in the west of Ireland in 1919. A piper called Ruane visited a place called Teach a Gheata (Gate House) every Sunday. In the words of a local man, Tomas Laighleis:

> *No old person, man or woman who had a hop in them failed to come. There was no fighting or trouble, no man was seen drunk there, no girl ever lost her reputation there.... The parish priest with one terrible sermon from the altar stopped them.*
>
> *Ruane was told what had happened and what the priest had said. He burst out crying, turned on his heel and went home. Ruane never came another Sunday there or any other piper ever again there.*

The priests were not always successful in their endeavours. Great care was taken not to let them know where and when a dance was happening, and look-outs would be posted on the road to warn the assembly to break up. But they made up for it by preaching fiery sermons. John Killourhy remembers from his own youth:

> *Well the old priests were a fright to God, I might as well tell you the truth. They were desperate. They were giving desperate sermons ... they were telling the people they were damned – they'll go down to Hell. The divil will drag them away without telling them they were damned.*

The dance music managed to resist this kind of extra-terrestrial pressure, and we can assume that not all priests felt so violently. Indeed many priests came from the same background as their parishioners, had grown up with the same music, and were even musicians themselves, so they probably turned a blind eye.

The house dances, patterns, and crossroad dances were the means by which the dance-music tradition was kept alive. Having survived the Famine, and clerical anathema, the death blow was nonetheless dealt to the tradition by a deadly combination of both Church and State.

In the twenties another dance craze hit Ireland. This craze was for 'modern' dancing like waltzes, foxtrots, and so on. The dances were held in commercial dance halls beyond the reach of clergy and moral watchdogs of any kind. The popularity of this kind of dancing incensed not only the clergy but other elements in society who saw in these 'foreign' dances a threat to the moral well-being of the entire youth of the country. By the 1930s both Church and government were denouncing dancing from pulpit, press, school, and political platforms. The Public Dance Halls Act of 1936 required all public dance halls to be licensed, and to operate under certain conditions. The priests used the Act as a way of finishing off the house dances, with the aid of the police.

In the thirties house dances would often be held in conjunction with raffles or card-game tournaments. This was the time of the Economic War in Ireland. Exports of farm produce to Britain were suspended and Irish farmers, especially small farmers were badly hit. The house dances or soirées as they were known were ways of raising money for people in the community who were in financial trouble. Suggestions that the proceeds were going to fund illegal organisations like the Irish Republican Army, and the priests' contention that they were occasions of sin led to their closure.

The legal pretext was that house dances constituted an infringement of the Public Dance Halls Act. Purely private house dances with no raffle or tournament aspect were also harried out of existence. Junior Crehan, a fiddle player from Co. Clare where house dances were very popular, remembers what happened then:

> *The clergy started to build the parochial halls to which all were expected to go and the Government collected 25 per cent of the ticket tax. In these halls modern dance bands played a different type of dancing – Foxtrot, One Step, and Shimmy Shake ... the dance halls were not natural places of enjoyment; they were not places for traditional music, story-telling and dancing; they were unsuitable for passing on traditional arts. The Dance Hall Act had closed our schools of tradition and left us a poorer people.*[9]

The priests' work was undoubtedly helped along by the emigration which started again after the First World War and continued unabated until the sixties. In addition, radio broadcasting had started and the gramophone had arrived. The house dances would have been affected by these developments in any event.

9 'Junior Crean
  Remembers', *Dal gCais*,
  1977

THE CÉILÍ BAND

Fortunately Irish dance music did not just disappear. It couldn't beat the dance halls so it joined them. The céilí band was born out of this compromise between modernity and tradition. The Irish word 'céilí' refers to the practice of gathering in a neighbour's house for chat, and story-telling, and sometimes, but not necessarily, dancing. The word can be used in English as an adjective as in céilí band or as a noun to describe an organised dance. These céilí were first organised by nationalist-minded emigrants in London at the beginning of the twentieth century. The idea was borrowed from Scottish revivalist groups who used to organise dances which featured settings of Scottish dances. The dances danced at these Irish céilí in England owed more to Scotland than to Ireland, resembling the group dances of that country and not the set and solo dances of the country-house dances.

Irish cultural activities were very popular with the Irish in Britain around this time, and there was also a lot of travelling between the two countries. Ireland, or at least twenty-six counties of it, had become an independent state, and in these conditions there was a revival of interest in Irish music and culture generally. So the prototype for what became the céilí band emerged amongst Irish emigrant groups in England and America and was then adopted in the home country. The classic line-up of a céilí band was fiddle, flute, accordion, piano and drums. The music, to adapt itself to the dance hall, had to become louder and have a heavier and more rhythmic backing. Many of the musicians were solo traditional players in their own right and competed as solo players at the Fleadheanna (traditional music competitions) which began in the fifties.

The céilí bands endured for forty years and although there are still céilí bands performing in Ireland today, their heyday is past. The céilí dances, group dances like 'The Walls of Limerick' and 'The Siege of Ennis' where the dancers faced each other in long lines, and the eight- and sixteen-hand reels have been replaced by the 'sets'. The sets are dances performed by four couples who dance as partners face to face, or facing out and holding hands. These correspond to the sets of the country-house dances and do not require a band.

Many purists decry the céilí bands as a sell-out. Many of the céilí were run by stridently nationalist and (ironically) Catholic groups. In many cases their objectives were not so much to provide music and entertainment as to preserve Irish youth from foreign 'immoral' influences. As the sixties and seventies approached, many young people were repelled or bored by céilí dancing.

Seán Ó Riada, whose work as a composer and innovator in the field of traditional music is described in detail in Chapter 7, thought the céilí band an abomination. His objections were musical:

> *The most important principles of traditional music – the whole idea of variation, the whole idea of the personal utterance – are abandoned. Instead everyone takes hold of a tune and belts away at it with as much relation to music as the buzzing of a bluebottle in an upturned jam jar.*[10]

Seán Ó Riada first voiced these harsh criticisms on a radio programme entitled 'Our Musical Heritage' in 1962. He had his own ideas about group-playing of Irish music, which he had already begun to put into practice. What he was doing would change the face of Irish traditional music radically. The reverberations of the impact are still felt today.

In defence of céilí bands Barry Taylor, in an article, 'Irish Céilídh Bands: A Break with Tradition?' has this to say:

> *[Ó Riada] had failed to understand the fundamental role of the music, and, therefore, of its practitioners. Any questions of 'personal utterance' and 'variation' are entirely secondary to the musicians' main role: that is to provide a solid rhythmic base for the dancers.*[11]

As one traditional player remarked, 'you didn't play to be listened to, you played to be danced to. . . . There was no such thing as a player coming into a house and expecting people to sit down, listening to him.'

It is true that the céilí bands kept dance music alive for dancers, brought it to a wider audience than otherwise would have been possible, and gave a platform and a training to young players.

10 Seán Ó Riada, *Our Musical Heritage*, p. 74

11 Barry Taylor, 'Irish Ceílídh Bands: A Break with Tradition?', *Dal gCais*, 1984

DANCING MUSIC/LISTENING MUSIC

God be good to Seamus Ennis, but if you danced when Seamus Ennis was playing you were soon told to stop, particularly by Seamus; this was music for listening even though it was dance music.

CIARÁN MACMATHÚNA[12]

Until the twentieth century the dance music of Ireland was played for community dancing, at house parties, patterns, weddings, wakes, and so on. The one exception to this rule was when a player of renowned virtuosity played. He, or more rarely she, was listened to. These players became, in Ciarán Mac Mathúna's words, 'musicians in their own right', no longer defined by the dance. They were exceptional though, and it was demanded of the rest that they perform for the dance.

In the 1920s a development took place which changed the relationship between musicians and dancers for ever. It happened in America and it had a profound effect on the future course of Irish traditional music both in Ireland and America. It was the invention of the gramophone or rather the Victrola as it was called. The recording companies in the United States cottoned on fast to the fact that there was an immigrant market to be exploited and wasted no time in signing up 'ethnic' musicians. (Irish musicians had recorded earlier than this on wax cylinders, many of which made their way back to Ireland, but the wax cylinders wore out eventually and the quality was much better on the 78 rpm discs issued in the twenties.)

In the following years hundreds of recordings of Irish traditional musicians were released and thousands of them made their way across the Atlantic. In the twenties Irish radio had begun broadcasting. One of the first acts to be featured was a traditional group called The Ballinakill Céilí Band. The process whereby music became separated from the dance had begun. It gathered momentum quickly until there was almost no traditional dancing going on in the country. The cultural significance of these events was momentous. Dancers and musicians were ambivalent about these developments:

12 Ciarán Mac Mathúna.

Interview, *BIABH*

13 John Killourhy,

Interview, *BIABH*

The only fault that was in the gramophone was you see – the dance! There was nice music alright in it; it was very lively very fast ... [but] it might stop before the figure was finished you see and they [the dancers] would have to stand up on the floor. So they preferred the musicians.

JOHN KILLOURHY[13]

THE STRAIN
OF THE DANCE

It would be true to say that over the period 1900 to 1950 most of the important developments in the field of Irish music that did happen took place in the USA.[1]

SEAMUS MAC MATHÚNA

The years after the Famine up until the late 1930s were important years for Irish traditional music, particularly for the instrumental or dance-music tradition. In those years over four million people left Ireland for America, and each ship that left carried with it a cargo of music. Irish music transplanted itself well in the new country, and by so doing ensured that it remained a living tradition. It renewed and changed itself in a way that affected the subsequent development of the music in its adopted country and the country of its birth.

The American-Irish tradition made two significant, life-giving contributions to Irish music. One was the collection of Irish music made by Captain Francis O'Neill, especially his *The Dance Music of Ireland*, subtitled *1001 Gems*.

The other was the 78 rpm record.

1 Seamus Mac Mathúna,

Treoir, 1987, Uimh. 1

IRISH DANCE MUSIC IN AMERICA

By 1850 twenty-six per cent of the population of New York, and twenty per cent of the population of Chicago was Irish born. By 1855 there were one and a half million Irish-born people living in America. Of the generation born in Ireland in 1831 only one in three died at home.

As we have seen, the Irish at this stage were crowded into shanty towns and living in miserable conditions, working at the most menial of jobs. To ease their way in the new country they attempted to transplant the customs and traditions of the society they had been born into. Music was highly regarded in that society and became a mainstay in the lives of the first generation of Irish emigrants to America. Irish traditional musicians were typical of the first Famine emigrants. As we have seen, they came from a rural background of subsistence farming and landless labourers, and they left Ireland in equal proportion. Many of the travelling pipers and 'professional' musicians lost their livelihood after the famine and followed their audience out to America.

They played at weddings, wakes and social gatherings. Some, as we have seen, made their way into music hall and variety then beginning to cater for an exclusively immigrant audience. Irish music went into the ethnic melting pot and eventually made up a part of an identifiably American form of popular entertainment, reaching its high point of expression in the character of George M. Cohan.

In places, the tradition remained intact. The old tunes and styles of playing gave expression and identity to an Irish community which was not in a big rush to become American. Life in nineteenth-century Chicago exemplifies this aspect of the Irish-American community and is embodied in the life of Captain Francis O'Neill.

'O'NEILL'S 1001'

Francis O'Neill was born in Tralibane, near Bantry in Co. Cork, in 1849. He was a clever student and an accomplished traditional flute player. He came from an area rich in traditional music and the O'Neill family home was open house to local and travelling musicians. O'Neill had a musical ear and a phenomenal memory. In his recollections of this time, he said that he never forgot any tune or song he ever heard.

Captain Francis O'Neill, author of one of the most famous collections of Irish traditional music – *The Dance Music of Ireland* – published in 1907

As I have mentioned, when he was still a child the parish priest of the area banned all crossroads and house dances. This had the effect of putting a stop to the playing of music altogether, and may have been a factor in young Francis's decision to leave home, which he did at the age of sixteen in 1865.

He did not go directly to America, but worked his passage on several ships, had many voyages, was shipwrecked and ended up in San Francisco. By 1871 he was in Chicago, where he was later sworn in as a policeman, rising to become Chief of Police in 1901.

But in that year of O'Neill's arrival in Chicago, the city was devastated by fire. The rebuilding of the city after the fire gave work to thousands of Irish immigrants and also gave them a strong position in the construction industry, which they still retain. The fire had broken out in the house of a Mrs O'Leary where an Irish fiddle player, Pat McLoughlin, was entertaining his newly-arrived Irish cousin at a party.

O'Neill became involved in Irish musical activities. There was a good demand for traditional music at the time, and there were many house parties, sessions, and functions. There were also dance halls and saloons which featured Irish music. O'Neill often found work for traditional musicians as policemen. The Chicago police force employed a disproportionately high percentage of traditional musicians while O'Neill was their chief. Typical of O'Neill was the recruitment of Barney Delaney, a saloon piper, a class of musician O'Neill did not entirely approve of. He realised, however, that Delaney was an exceptional musician and persuaded him to join the force.

O'Neill had an active association with traditional musicians through the Chicago Irish Music Club, at informal house sessions and with celebrated professional Irish musicians, like Patsy Touhey, who passed through the city. He realised the high quality of the music being played in America, and set about collecting tunes with the help of his friend James O'Neill.

The Chicago Music Club. Organisations of Irish musicians were established in the late nineteenth century in America to preserve traditional music and to provide opportunities for playing

A sergeant on the force, James O'Neill was a fiddle player who could write music, unlike Captain O'Neill. Initially, Captain O'Neill made the twenty-mile journey to Sergeant O'Neill's house and simply played everything he could remember. The sergeant then transcribed the tune in staff notation. Gradually other musicians became involved and their tunes were included in the collection. At this stage there was no intention to publish. The objective was to preserve the music.

The collection also included tunes and airs culled from old manuscripts and printed sources which were considered worthy of note. A vast amount of material – nearly 2000 pieces – was notated and the decision was then taken to publish. In 1903 1850 pieces were presented for publication under the title, *The Music of Ireland*. Hundreds of dance tunes which had never been seen in print before appeared in this book. There were some hundred song airs too which had not previously been collected.

O'Neill decided to publish some settings of airs which had come from other collections, notably those of Edward Bunting, and George Petrie. Bunting and Petrie had made their collections from the late eighteenth to the mid-nineteenth centuries. Neither had a background in traditional music as O'Neill had, nor were they traditional musicians as he was. These collections were the work of antiquarians as much as anything else, and had been presented to an educated and literate middle-class audience.

Of collectors like Bunting and Petrie, another great Irish collector Breandán Breathnach said: 'They deserved to be honoured and remembered for their labours but their work might remain undisturbed on library shelves without any harm being done thereby to the living tradition.'[2]

The publication of O'Neill's *Music of Ireland* marked the first collection made by a practitioner for the use and interest of other practitioners. This achievement ensured that dance music which otherwise would have disappeared was preserved and remained part of a living tradition.

In 1907 O'Neill published another volume entitled *The Dance Music of Ireland* subtitled, *1001 Gems*. This book has been known ever since as *O'Neill's 1001*, containing, as it does, exactly that number of dance tunes.

The first book had been criticised on the grounds that O'Neill had 'lifted' tunes found in other collections, and had included non-traditional material such as Moore's melodies and 'Irish' airs by contemporary composers. In this volume he excluded

2 Breandán Breathnach, *The Use of Notation in the Transmission of Irish Folk Music* (UCC, 1986), p. 2

everything except dance tunes. Amongst players the book was very well received and he was praised for the quality of the tune settings and selections.

O'Neill's *Dance Music of Ireland* is still used by traditional musicians. It has never been surpassed and it is quite common for musicians to refer to 'The Book' as the source for tunes which they are including in their performance. O'Neill's book was also a landmark in that it marked an important early stage in the standardisation of Irish traditional music. 'The Book' came back to Ireland, and was used by traditional players. Inevitably it made inroads on the local repertoire. O'Neill collected tunes from immigrant Irish musicians who came from every part of Ireland. No one complete regional style could therefore be represented. There is a preponderance of reels (350), for example, which did not reflect the situation in every district, where jigs, slides, or polkas might have been more popular. The collection is an amalgam of all Irish dance music, and what it provided then was the basis for a national repertoire as opposed to a plethora of regional ones.

It is also important to understand that traditional musicians do not use the book, in the way a classical musician would play directly from a score. The notated music is just the skeleton or melody line of the tune. It's also identified as a jig, reel, hornpipe or whatever. Remember these tunes were notated from the playing, humming, or lilting of a musician, yet they give no indication of the ornamentation employed by the performer. The grace notes, rolls, slides, etc. are left out. The musician in performance will fill them in. In a later book, *Waifs and Strays of Gaelic Melody*, O'Neill points out that 'to illustrate the wealth of graces, turns and trills, which adorn the performance of capable Irish pipers and fiddlers, skilful both in execution and improvisation, is beyond the scope of musical notation'.[3]

Even if it were within the scope of notation to do such a thing it would undermine the whole basis of traditional playing. We have seen how this relies on the skill and imagination of the individual performer who is free to improvise and ornament a tune.

Sergeant O'Neill, in making his transcriptions, had sometimes altered tunes to fit in with the classical scale system in which he had been trained. So what use is O'Neill's *Dance Music of Ireland* or any notated music for that matter in the playing of traditional music?

3 Cit. Breathnach in Preface to O'Neill, *Irish Minstrels and Musicians* (Mercier Press, Cork, 1987)

Staff notation mostly serves a two fold purpose for traditional players. It elucidates a twist or turn in a tune which his ear has failed to pick up: it recalls to memory a tune once played but now forgotten. Here the notation may be likened to a photograph – the features in both cases are instantly recalled on sight and the notation and the photograph can ... be dispensed with. Memory takes over as the original impression reinstates itself.[4]

New tunes are also learned from staff notation by some traditional players. In this way O'Neill provided future generations of players with a treasure house of Irish dance tunes – of musical photographs. His contribution remains one of the most significant in the recent history of the tradition.

ADAPTING TO THE AMERICAN WAY OF LIFE

In the Chicago of O'Neill's time there were several dance halls, and dancing also took place on social occasions like weddings. By the late 1880s, the distinction was being made between music for dance and music for listening. O'Neill was actively involved in the Chicago Music Club which was primarily an organisation of players. The provision of music for dancing was not the only item on its agenda. The members were interested in the music for itself, and were happy to play for each other, without the presence of dancers.

Travelling shows like Jerry Cohan's *Hibernicon* often featured an 'Irish piper' who played on the stage in a concert setting. Organisations like the Gaelic League, interested in promoting Irish cultural events, mounted concerts of Irish traditional music for a seated, middle-class, Irish-American audience.

O'Neill himself made a distinction between two great pipers of the day, Barney Delaney and Patsy Touhey, proving the dancing/listening distinction well established. Barney Delaney, he declared: 'Has no equal as a player for dancers, both in time, swing and execution. Touhey is regarded by some as a better player – he probably is ... but not for a dancer.'

Dancing in Ireland took place on a small scale, groups of neighbours at crossroads, or in barns. A single musician was adequate to the needs of the dancers in this context. In commercial dance halls, in noisy American cities, it was important that the musician or musicians could be heard. The uilleann pipes, for example, were adapted to American conditions by

The dance hall in immigrant communities has always been a major social centre in America. It was the place where people recently arrived ... met people who were already there. Courtships took place there, it was a social centre ... and music and dancing were always interrelated there.
MICK MOLONEY[5]

4 Breandán Breathnach,
  The Use of Notation
5 Mick Moloney,
  Interview, *BIABH*

two Irish pipe-makers, Billy and Charley Taylor. They were the same pitch, established as concert pitch, the key of D. The Taylors modified the bore of the chanter (the flute-like part which plays the melody) to give a much louder sound. The pipes needed to be heard from a concert platform, or in a crowded dance hall.

There is an account of piper Patsy Touhey, a famous performer of that time, playing for a crowd of five hundred dancers at a Gaelic League function in 1901 in Springfield, Massachusetts. It is hard to imagine in these days of amplification how this could have been audible. Now, it is common practice to mike all the sounding parts of the uilleann pipes for performances to crowds much smaller than five hundred people. People, moreover, are listening, not dancing. Of this same event in Springfield, it was reported in the *Irish World* newspaper, most of the evening was given up to 'Irish jigs, reels, hornpipes, and "sets" as danced in Ireland'.

The Gaelic League was a self-consciously Irish movement devoted to the revival of Gaelic culture and a supporter of the Irish nationalist movement. It drew, for its support on the better-off sections of Irish-American society, the emerging middle classes. It was a successful organisation in this regard and large numbers attended the various functions and concerts held under its auspices. It had the whole-hearted support of musicians like Patsy Touhey and Francis O'Neill who saw in the Gaelic League the means of keeping traditional music and culture alive in America.

The Gaelic League did have an important long-term effect on dancing, which in a way consolidated the division between it and the music. Through the organised functions of the League, a very formalised kind of group dancing emerged which was far removed from the country 'set' dances of Irish social life.

The group dances of nineteenth-century Ireland were for the most part based on quadrilles. A quadrille is a figure dance of four couples; its name derives from the square made by the four couples. These dances maintained their popularity for well over a hundred years, and are undergoing a major revival at the moment. Because they are truly social dances, sets can be got up with groups as small as two couples (the half set) and can be accommodated in private houses, pubs, and so on; anywhere in fact where there is a musician who knows how to play for dancers. The dances organised by the Gaelic League were more formal, and took place in halls and hotels. The

League devised dances where long lines of dancers, girls on one side and boys on the other, faced each other, and danced steps to Irish jigs, reels, and so on. Figures developed which involved skipping in and out and linking arms and so on. Authentic group dances were introduced also in 1898 under the instructions of dancing masters. As we have seen, eventually this type of dancing came to be known as céilí dancing.

Later still, dances which were not Irish – like the waltz – were adapted to Irish tunes and added to the repertoire. This happened first in Britain where there was a substantial Irish community, and then in America and Ireland. Old style set dancing was ultimately eclipsed to be replaced by céilí dancing.

Despite the best efforts of musicians and activists like O'Neill and the Gaelic League to keep the music alive and untainted, the second generation began to lose interest. Very few of the children of the Chicago Irish Music Club members played traditional music, and the society died out in the twenties.

The changes taking place in the Irish-American community in Chicago were mirrored in the other cities of East-Coast America. By 1900 only thirty-three per cent of five million Irish-Americans were Irish born. The Catholic church in Chicago, as in other cities, had always encouraged the Irish to assimilate by becoming good American citizens. Respect for authority, particularly Church authority, and the inculcation of the work ethic were high on the Church's agenda. They wanted their congregations to shed the stereotypes imposed on them by WASP (White Anglo-Saxon Protestant) America.

Father Andrew Greely, an American sociologist and writer, says: 'The bigotry of these crude images haunted Irish Americans for generations. Irish clergy, eager to push the acculturation of their people, refused to baptise girl children Brigid ... because of the negative connotations the name had acquired ... and Nora was converted into Elanor at baptism because the former was "too Irish".'[6]

From 1845, the Catholic Church in America had radically reorganised itself, centralised its administration, increased the supply of Irish priests, and engaged in massive building programmes. Francis O'Neill blamed the decline of Irish music and culture on the clergy's failure to promote it: 'Religious organisations, propaganda and church extension ... monopolize the interests of our race. Every organised effort not affiliated with the church or encouraged by the clergy seems doomed.'[7] He was very pessimistic about the future of Irish music in America and wrote to a friend in Ireland in 1918 that:

6 Preface to Appel, *Patriots to Patriots*

7 Cit. Breathnach in Preface to O'Neill, *Irish Minstrels and Musicians* (Mercier Press, Cork, 1987).

'Few of our people care a snap for Irish music. The poor scrub who graduated from the pick and shovel and the mother who toiled for many years in some Yankee kitchen will have nothing less for Katie and Gladis or Jimmy and Raymond but the very latest.'[8]

As Mick Moloney sees it:

> *There was a kind of ambivalence in their attitude to their culture: on the one hand they loved the dance hall, they loved the old music and they loved being Irish. On the other hand they wanted to shed the negative images coming from an oppressed peasant culture, and embedded in the culture itself was the dance music ... They felt proud of their culture and ... they felt ashamed. So you found that even as the dance music was flourishing, at the same time it was going into a decline.*[9]
>
> MICK MOLONEY

Ambivalence and lack of church support were not the only factors to account for the fall-off in interest in Irish culture. The old city neighbourhoods, enclaves of the Irish, were being abandoned in favour of the suburbs. The mobility of American life could not support a music culture which was based on continuity.

O'Neill was over-pessimistic as it turned out. Even at the time he was writing, the first commercial recordings of Irish traditional music were beginning to appear. This was to give the tradition a shot in the arm in America and Ireland, thereby providing a place for it in the urbanised, industrialised world of the twentieth century.

DANCE MUSIC ON RECORD

> *My mother owned a record store in Manhattan, and Irish people were always coming in and asking for old favorites, like 'The Stack of Barley'. Well she'd no records to give them because there weren't any. So she sent me up to Gaelic Park in the Bronx to find some musicians. There was always music there on Sundays. Well I found Eddie Herborn and John Whelan playing banjo and accordion, and they sounded great. So my mother went to Columbia, and they said that if she would agree to buy five hundred copies from them they would record Herborn and Wheeler. She agreed and they both recorded 'The Stack of Barley' and the five hundred records sold out in no time at all.*
>
> JUSTUS O'BYRNE DEWITT[10]

8 Ibid., Preface

9 Mick Moloney.
   Interview, *BIABH*

10 Justus O'Byrne DeWitt
   in Mick Moloney, 'Irish
   Ethnic Recordings' in
   *Ethnic Recordings in
   America – A Neglected
   Heritage* (American
   Folklife Center Library
   of Congress, 1982), p. 90

This was an auspicious moment in Irish recording history. From 1916 when the Columbia company made this first recording of a popular Irish dance tune until the late thirties thousands of recordings of Irish dance music were made.

There had been recordings of Irish music made before this, but on the Edison phonograph. This machine recorded on to wax cylinders but it was not possible to make more than one copy of the recording at a time. Patsy Touhey bought an Edison machine in about 1900 for recording, thereby bypassing the commercial recording companies. He made many recordings of his own playing which he sold by mail order. Several of these found their way to Ireland, and are still in existence.

Flat-disc recordings eventually took over from the phonograph. Hundreds of duplicates could be taken from one master. Initially gramophone manufactures like the Victor company were looking for a way to sell their machines. They realised that there was a huge market to be exploited in the immigrant communities. 'So,' Mick Moloney says, 'they basically started what has now been called the A & R business; they would employ people in that community to record people ... that would be popular enough for people to want to buy their records, and to want to buy their gramophones – so it was a circular thing'.[11]

There was a thriving Irish dance scene in the main Irish American cities in the twenties. It was to the bands and musicians who played in the bars and dance halls that the recording companies went in search of talent. A flurry of recording activity ensued.

Two recording artists of these years between the two world wars deserve special mention. These were two fiddle-players from Co. Sligo, Michael Coleman and James Morrison.

Coleman and Morrison, the two most important Sligo players of this period, were born within miles of each other. Coleman, born in 1891, emigrated to America in 1914 and Morrison, born in 1893, went there in the early twenties. Their recordings set the course of Irish traditional music for the next fifty years.

They played in the Sligo regional style, typically highly ornamented, and fast, with a fluid bowing style. The effect of this style has been described as 'jaunty' and 'flamboyant'. It was, and remains, a very attractive style of playing, and in the hands of Coleman and Morrison literally superseded all other styles of playing. Both were virtuoso players of great technical skill. Coleman in particular is considered by some to be superior in the matter of 'setting a tune'. His recordings are still listened

I think it is clear that a largely standardised style of playing Irish traditional music held sway for a long period in the mid part of this century. The main elements of this style were the repertoire as provided in O'Neill's books and the mode of playing as exemplified by the great Sligo players featured on 78's in America.
JACKIE SMALL[12]

11 Mick Moloney. Interview, *BIABH*
12 Jackie Small. Interview, *BIABH*

Fiddler James Morrison from Co. Sligo, one of the most influential Irish musicians to be recorded in America

to and admired by traditional musicians and music lovers, as are Morrison's.

The Coleman and Morrison recordings came back to Ireland in their thousands, where they had an extraordinary impact. In remote rural areas where regional styles and repertoires dominated, it became almost imperative to play in the Sligo style as exemplified by Morrison and Coleman. This involved not only playing like them, i.e., imitating their technique and ornamentation, but also playing their repertoire. As a result, local styles of playing, tunes and tune settings went out of fashion.

Reels predominated over jigs and hornpipes. Slides, polkas, mazurkas, schottisches, and highlands got little if any airing. The movement towards standardisation had started with O'Neill's *Dance Music of Ireland*. The emulation of Coleman and Morrison consolidated this. In Ireland and America versions and settings of tunes were played in the order selected by

Coleman and Morrison on the original recordings: 'Even yet,' writes Seamus MacMathúna, 'more than thirty years after Coleman's death ... one seldom hears "Bonny Kate" without "Jenny's Chickens". "Tarbolton" is inevitably followed by "The Longford Collector" and "The Sailor's Bonnet". Compare any old recording of either of these two players with recent recordings of traditional music and this will be borne out.'[13]

Musicians were now learning tunes and techniques from records, as well as from players, and this practice has persisted. Non-players now had gramophone recordings of musicians who had achieved standards of excellence which local musicians could not hope to match. Irish traditional music became a performance art, to be listened to on record or in concert. There are many accounts of the excitement with which a new batch of records from America was greeted. Frankie Gavin, fiddle-player with De Danann, acknowledges the influence on his playing of these recordings. His father who 'played a bit on the fiddle' was also very impressed: 'Religiously every Saturday he went into Galway when he was a younger chap, on his bike and his mother gave him the price of a 78 ... he ... had a huge collection.... Coleman was my father's favourite.'[14]

James Morrison is Frankie's favourite and, as he says himself, 'the approach he had to fiddle playing and the approach he had to any tune he touched just ... can't be beaten ... nobody can play like that today. I work towards trying to recreate that in my own playing.' Frankie is a virtuoso player in his own right, yet Morrison, dead for more than forty years, is to him the consummate fiddle player. This is a measure of his achievement. There are others who hold Coleman in equal regard. The musician Seamus Mac Mathúna recalls the effect Coleman's playing had on an Irish 'exile' in New York in the thirties, who 'wept with sheer joy on hearing Coleman playing "Lord McDonald": "It cannot be, it cannot be" he repeated, "no earthly man could make music like that".'[15]

The effect of these recordings of Coleman, Morrison and others was to popularise Irish traditional music especially in Ireland where it had gone into a decline for reasons outlined in Chapter 5. Moreover, they set high standards for aspiring traditional players. They also revived an interest in and respect for traditional music in areas where it had died out. It was a source of some pride that a musical form associated with poverty and peasant culture had attained such acclaim. This all was to the benefit of Irish music.

There were some negative effects too. The universal adoption

13 Seamus Mac Mathúna, 'Coleman, Morrison and Killoran', *Treoir*, 1987, Uimh. 1

14 Frankie Gavin. Interview, *BIABH*

15 Seamus Mac Mathúna, 'Coleman, Morrison and Killoran'

Frankie Kennedy (flute)
and Mairéad Ní
Mhaonaigh (fiddle), both
are members of the
contemporary traditional
band Altan

of the Sligo style and repertoire, as exemplified by Coleman and Morrison and other players recording in America, downgraded regional playing. The wide variety of regional styles and tunes had enriched the tradition. Some, not all of this, lost out to the standardisation imposed by American recordings. Areas like Sliabh Luachra and Donegal resisted most of the influence of the recordings and kept their musical identity.

Today the wheel has come full circle and musicians like Mairéad Ní Mhaonaigh from Donegal are looking to regional styles as a source: 'we rooted down . . . and went for the very old tunes and what the local men were playing'. Mairéad and the band Altan, of which she is a member, recorded for *Bringing It All Back Home* two highlands followed by two reels. All the tunes originate in Donegal except for one highland, 'Neil Gow's', which is a seventeenth-century import from Scotland. Altan do not recreate the old Donegal style; they reinterpret it, using the tunes and techniques associated with it. They are a contemporary traditional band, playing in an ensemble style, and incorporating instruments like the guitar, which is a very recent addition to Irish music. They would acknowledge many influences on their style of playing, but Donegal is an important element in their music.

The dance-music tradition is alive and well, both in America and in Ireland, and the American recordings of the twenties and thirties played no small part in this. It also seems from the interest in set dancing which has now reached America that the dance is returning to the music. Step- or exhibition-dancing has long been popular in America, but this is concentrated exclusively on competition and young dancers. Set dancing involves young and old, and affords a wide range of people the possibility of expressing themselves through traditional music in social situations.

It is unlikely that Irish instrumental music will ever again be played exclusively for dancing. The music now endures as a thing in itself to be enjoyed and experienced by players and listeners alike.

CHAPTER SEVEN

SEÁN Ó RIADA

It's not often that a single person,

however gifted, can alter the

character of a nation's culture.

Ó Riada managed to do this.[1]

THOMAS KINSELLA

Ó RIADA AND IRISH TRADITIONAL MUSIC

The great age of American recording of Irish music ended in the late 1930s. The next breakthrough in Irish traditional music occurred in Ireland. One man in particular responded to the challenge presented to Irish music by the twentieth century. His name was Seán Ó Riada. He was a man for all seasons; a composer trained in the art music of Europe who immersed himself in the oral music tradition of Ireland.

He was exercised all his life by the question of Irish cultural identity, especially but not exclusively concerned with cultural expression through music. He found new ways for the music to express itself: in orchestral settings, film programme music, and liturgical and choral singing.

Guided by his vision, traditional music changed radically, and became accessible to a modern Irish audience, and through this traditional music the cultural life of Ireland was invigorated. The consequences of Ó Riada's work were far reaching: contemporary, classical, folk, and rock musicians of recent years, who have chosen to work with Irish idioms, cite him as a creative source in their work; generations of Irish people are indebted to him for restoring to them their nation's music.

1 Thomas Kinsella,
  Preface, Seán Ó Riada,
  Our Musical Heritage,
  p. 9

Seán Ó Riada playing the
Bodhrán – a traditional
Irish hand drum

EARLY YEARS

Typical of many of his generation, Seán Ó Riada was one generation removed from a farming background: his mother had left the countryside to become a nurse and his father a policeman. Born in 1931, he was known until his early twenties by the English version of his name, John Reidy. Both parents were musical, and he learned to play the traditional fiddle as a child.

It was apparent early on that he was musically and intellectually gifted. As a student at University College, Cork, where he changed his studies from Classics to music, he had a wide range of cultural interests: Greek literature, French culture, playing jazz and listening to European avant-garde music.

After graduating he became assistant musical director in Radio Eireann, the national broadcasting service. A few years later, in 1955, he moved to the Abbey Theatre as musical director. (The Abbey Theatre is the national theatre of Ireland, founded in 1904 by the poet W. B. Yeats and Lady Gregory.) Through his work with the Abbey he renewed his acquaintance with Irish traditional music.

Required to arrange some traditional pieces for a play there, he decided to augment the theatre orchestra with traditional players. The orchestra players were classically trained, and he felt that for the music to be authentic it should be played in the traditional manner. This led him into the company of traditional musicians living in Dublin. Through them he came to consider the creative possibilities of traditional music.

The status of traditional music in the 1950s in Ireland was low. It was confined mainly to the rural areas of the country, or to Irish-language revivalist groups, or to a small coterie of traditional players living in the cities. The broad mass of the Irish public had little connection with its traditional music.

Unlike many European countries Ireland never experienced a strong art-music movement centred around its traditional music. These movements turned the focus away from traditional music to classical. In the process, classical art music came to be an expression of national culture. There are many examples: Chopin in Poland, Smetana in Czechoslovakia, Grieg in Norway, Sibelius in Finland.

Ó Riada had been classically trained in the idiom of European art music, but was very conscious that this music was not native to Ireland. Irish musical expression was traditional. He was also aware that traditional music was in danger of disappearing unless Irish people were reintroduced to it in a way that was meaningful.

One of the tasks Ó Riada set himself was to find a suitable setting in which to present the music, without compromising it. 'He thought that he needed to do something dramatic to make people take notice of it. So he decided the best thing to do would be to put it in the same sort of atmosphere as classical music ... in other words, on stage, in a concert even though it didn't suit the music itself, which he did ... in about 1959.'[2]

CEOLTÓIRÍ CHUALANN

Concert halls and theatres were the setting. Ensemble playing was the vehicle.

Ceoltóirí Chualann were the group of traditional musicians Ó Riada gathered together who were entrusted with the mission of restoring Irish traditional music to popular appeal. Under his direction they achieved this objective.

2 Peadar Ó Riada, Interview, *BIABH*

Group playing was not a new thing. Céilí bands consisting of traditional players with the additional backing of piano, accordion and drums, had been around for nearly thirty years. Céilí bands were anathema to Ó Riada. To him they represented the most debased form of Irish traditional music.

Ceoltóirí Chualann was to be 'an ideal type of Céilí Band' or Folk Orchestra. The principle of variation would be expressed by:

> *stating the basic skeleton of the tune to be played; this then would be ornamented and varied by solo instruments, or by small groups of solo instruments. The more variation the better, so long as it has roots in the tradition, and serves to extend that tradition.*[3]

3 Seán Ó Riada, *Our Musical Heritage*, p. 74

Seán Ó Riada (harpsichord) with Ceoltóirí Chualann at the Gaiety Theatre, Dublin in 1969. The dress suits were worn at Ó Riada's insistence

These ideas were worked out and articulated in a series of radio programmes Ó Riada presented in 1962, under the title *Our Musical Heritage*. Ceoltóirí Chualann was the musical expression of these ideas.

Some of the concerts given by Ó Riada and Ceoltóirí Chualann were recorded and are still available on disc, and these recordings give some idea of the atmosphere of excitement.

The music is played with great verve, rhythm and feeling, and the personality of Ó Riada shines through. The repertoire was Irish dance music, airs, and the compositions of Carolan and the older harpers. Ceoltóirí Chualann also featured a singer Seán Ó Sé, who was a tenor. Seán Ó Sé's singing style and the accompaniment devised by Ó Riada was yet another innovation.

At one memorable concert, in Dublin's Gaiety Theatre in March 1969, Ó Riada produced a new piece, a song entitled 'Mná na hEireann' (Women of Ireland). The music composed by Ó Riada was to accompany an eighteenth-century poem by Peadar Ó Doirnín, whose bicentenary was the occasion for the concert. Ó Riada's music for 'Mná na hEireann' resurfaced recently on a hit single released by a British group, The Christians.

MISE EIRE

In 1960 Ó Riada was commissioned to write the music for a film called *Mise Eire* (I am Ireland). *Mise Eire* documented through the use of archive material (some of which had never been seen before) Ireland's progress from British colony to nation state. Ó Riada used the great traditional song airs of Ireland as the basis of his programme music, which was scored for orchestra.

The film and the music took Ireland by storm. Ireland had no established film industry at the time and *Mise Eire* and its score were a source of great pride to the Irish public. It made Ó Riada a household name, and raised the status of Irish music amongst a section of society who had never taken any interest in it before.

You had, if you like ... a sophisticated middle-class audience who would go to symphony concerts played by symphony orchestras. Now they were listening to fantastic (Irish) music played by symphony orchestras. So Ó Riada did popularise Irish traditional music in that way.[4]

4 Ciarán Mac Mathúna,
Interview, *BIABH*

These were exciting times. Peadar Ó Riada, Seán's son recalls that his grandmother, Seán's mother, was

> *scared stiff in case it wouldn't work. The première was at the Cork Film Festival ... she was invited but she refused to go, in case he'd make a bags of it! But then her impatience got the better of her and she got her hat and stick and gloves ... and went down to Patrick Street. When she got off the bus she could hear the newspaper boys whistling the tune of* Mise Eire *so she knew it was a success. She just turned back on the next bus and came back to her husband and said 'the boy's done fine'.*[5]

Mise Eire was originally conceived as the first of a trilogy of films. The second film *Saoirse?* (Freedom?) was made and the music scored by Ó Riada; the third was never commissioned.

His last film commission in 1963 was the music for a screen adaptation of Synge's play *The Playboy of the Western World*.

Peggy Jordan, who organised folk and traditional concerts in Dublin at the time, remembers the excitement generated by Ó Riada's music: 'the music in that [film] is beautiful; the music sold that film more than the film did ... it put the music on another level and it excited everybody. Ó Riada meant an awful lot to me and to everybody I think because ... his music was so uplifting.'[6]

The next move Ó Riada made was geographical. He moved his family out of Dublin to the west Cork 'Gaeltacht', or Irish-speaking area, of Cúil Aodha. His house at Galloping Green, then a small village on the edge of Dublin city, was a meeting place for traditional musicians, many of whom were Irish speakers. Ó Riada was a gifted linguist and within a short space of time he and his wife Ruth made Irish the spoken language of the family.

Around this time he also adopted the Irish version of his name Seán Ó Riada. There was more than an element of re-invention about this process and a lesser man might not have brought it off. The mixture in Ó Riada of a strong sense of vision, great talent and intelligence, and showmanship provided all that was necessary for such an undertaking. He gave himself totally to the enterprise and the move to Cúil Aodha was consistent with everything he thought and did. He needed to return to the cultural origins of traditional music; he wanted to participate in that culture and he wanted to renew the music at its source.

5 Peadar Ó Riada.
  Interview, *BIABH*
6 Peggy Jordan,
  Interview, *BIABH*

PADDY KILLOURHY

LIAM O'FLYNN

CLANCY BROTHERS

PETE SEEGER

EVERLY BROTHERS

VAN MORRISON

U2

SINÉAD O'CONNOR

THE POGUES

THE WATERBOYS

CÚIL AODHA

> *At one stage my father decided when I was about six or seven years old, that he wanted to rear his family in the Gaeltacht ... he had no job of course, because he threw everything up at the time; just marched in one morning about eleven o'clock and said to my mother 'We're going, I can't stand the city life any more' ... a job was advertised in University College Cork, which he got, as music lecturer, and ... the nearest Gaeltacht was Cúil Aodha.*[7]

Cúil Aodha is a small village in the mountain region of west Cork near the Kerry border. Ó Riada bought a house there on the banks of the Sulan river, a stone's throw from his own mother's birthplace. She too had been a musician, an accomplished fiddle and concertina player.

A further auspicious coincidence lay in the fact that when he was a music student in University College, Cork, he had produced a setting of a song from the Cúil Aodha area called 'The Banks of Sulan'. This setting is still in the repertoire of the Radio Telefís Eireann Symphony Orchestra, the Irish national orchestra. Peadar, Seán's son, now lives in Cúil Aodha with his young family. 'When we landed here', he says, 'probably the house nearest the river was our house on the banks of Sulan; it's peculiar that we returned home, as it were, to the place where his musical thing came from originally.'

Traditional singer Nóirín Ní Riain sings with the Benedictine monks of Glenstal Abbey, Co. Limerick

7 Peadar Ó Riada. Interview, *BIABH*

The Second Vatican Council changed the liturgy of the Catholic Mass in 1964, and provided Ó Riada with further opportunities to extend traditional music into popular favour. Until these changes the Catholic mass had been celebrated in Latin. The musical liturgy of the Missa Cantata and the Latin hymns had grown up around this.

Now in the sixties it became possible to have mass celebrated in the vernacular language. In Ireland this was English in the main, but mass was celebrated in Irish in the Gaeltachts. For the first time in several hundred years the congregation played an active role in the celebration of mass by saying prayers, singing hymns and responses. The priest faced the congregation instead of the altar as before.

Ó Riada for his part composed a mass in Irish based on the 'Sean Nós' singing tradition. It was adopted by the Catholic church in Ireland and even in English-speaking parishes where there was usually one Irish language mass every Sunday.

Ó Riada composed two more masses and enjoyed very much teasing out a connection he perceived between 'Sean Nós' singing and plain chant. He had many lively discussions with his friends the Benedictine monks of Glenstal Abbey on this issue, about which they were not convinced but interested. (*Bringing It All Back Home* recorded the monks of Glenstal singing two Irish hymns 'An tAiséirí' and 'The Darkest Midnight' with traditional singer Nóirín Ní Riain.)

Ó Riada's mass has never been replaced in the liturgy of the mass in Irish. It was estimated that as many as ninety-six per cent of Irish Catholics in the sixties attended Sunday mass. By providing liturgical music of this kind, he ensured that the cadences and idioms of traditional singing remain familiar to Irish ears.

He also established a male voice choir in Cúil Aodha, which sang, and still sings in the church each Sunday, and feast day. In addition to singing religious works, the choir had a repertoire of traditional songs, and Ó Riada travelled with the members around the country to festivals and cultural events. These proliferated in the sixties. It was a time of heightened political consciousness in the Gaeltacht. There were many organisations established to pressurise the government for improved educational and social facilities and to provide better employment opportunities. Irish-language programmes on television highlighted the issues and also provided a public space for Irish cultural activities in which Seán Ó Riada participated. He was seen by many as a sort of cultural ambassador for the Cúil

Aodha Gaeltacht and assiduously lobbied on behalf of people there. Ceoltóirí Chualann and Cór Cúil Aodha played leading roles in this renaissance and renewal of tradition. Central to it was the dynamic force of Ó Riada's personality.

By establishing the choir and basing himself in Cúil Aodha, he placed himself in a position from which he could explore and develop a dimension of the tradition which Peadar identifies as 'the deeper thing, the spiritual thing underneath ... that's what he wanted to research more than anything else'.

Music and musical performance in places like Cúil Aodha cannot be equated with music in the concert or gig sense. A musical event, a gathering which may often take place in a pub, is usually described as a 'session' ('seisiún' in Irish). There is no payment, there is no programme, no set starting or finishing time, no stage and no audience. 'The premise of our culture', Peadar says, 'as a reflection in our music and poetry is that all of us must participate ... there is no audience.'

As well as throwing himself into the cultural life of Cúil Aodha and working with the tradition on the ground, Ó Riada worked hard at his new job in the music department of the university at Cork. He made a powerful impact on his students, as a teacher and also as a man of great charm, wit and personality. He brought traditional music into an atmosphere where before it had been of small importance. It was considered in the past little more than a source of melodies for arrangements.

The uilleann piper Tomás Ó Cannainn describes Ó Riada's attraction as a teacher in the preface to *Our Musical Heritage*: 'Sean's study of Irish tunes having their own internal logic ... led him ... to encourage his final year students at University College, Cork to use this motivic method in composition. Many of us found it a stimulating experience.' .

INSTRUMENTS AND INNOVATION

Ó Riada's intellectual curiosity and interests spread over the whole spectrum of Irish music. One of these interests was old Irish harp music. The problem was how best to represent it in performance when there were no old-style harpers or harps left. He hated the sound of the gut-strung modern harp which he associated with a debased kind of Irish parlour music.

Ó Riada resurrected Irish harp music from the old collections and began working it into the repertoire of Ceoltóirí Chualann. His innovation here was the introduction of a harpsichord, which he played himself. He felt that the sound of this instrument was true to the spirit of Irish harping and harp music even though it was a European instrument. This was a controversial view and the harpsichord was tolerated, perhaps in some cases because it was Ó Riada who was playing it. I have written more about Ó Riada and the harpsichord in Chapter 12.

The bodhrán was not an instrument much in evidence in traditional music in the twentieth century.

Its principal association was with the 'wren boys' or mummers who dressed up in fancy dress on St Stephen's Day and went around the local parish collecting money and playing music.

It is an Irish hand drum usually made of goatskin which is played with the hand or with a small wooden stick. Its appearance is that of a large tambourine and its original function seems to have been some kind of crude sieve used to separate the wheat from the chaff. The player balances the bodhrán on one knee holding it upright with the left hand, while the right hand plays (reversed if the player is left-handed).

Seán Ó Riada introduced the bodhrán into Ceoltóirí Chualann. Bodhrán player Peadar Mercier remembers: 'I think he liked the rhythm of it; he liked the compelling attraction of it and he played it with tremendous skill ... he led the group with the bodhrán and that's the one and only time the bodhrán took pride of place over the total ensemble.'

Ó Riada devoted quite a lot of attention to it in his radio series *Our Musical Heritage*: 'Altogether the versatility of this instrument, the variety of timbres produced by playing on the rim or on the skin, by playing with the stick or with the hand, and the variety of pitch available, make it a most suitable instrument for accompanying Irish music, particularly in a band.'[8] The bodhrán has since become virtually indispensable to the ensemble playing of Irish music. It is at home in traditional, folk, rock 'n' roll performance; in the orchestral music of Mícheál Ó Súilleabháin and the experimental soundscapes of the American composer John Cage.

The Irish musician Donal Lunny who has been interested in the rhythmic possibilities of the bodhrán for many years explains the attraction of hand drums over drum kits for Irish music: 'percussion in the sense of hand drums suits Irish music better than kit playing ... somehow the running qualities of

8 Seán Ó Riada *Our Musical Heritage*, p. 77

9 Donal Lunny. Interview, BIABH

10 Ciarán Mac Mathúna. Interview, *BIABH*

Irish tunes are best reinforced and embellished with hand drums and continuous rhythm.'[9]

Ó Riada wore many hats in his lifetime; one was that of the European art-music composer. From the late fifties to the mid-sixties he worked at classical composition, in addition to his other work. He died in 1971 at the tragically young age of forty and it is not clear what direction his life would have subsequently taken. He had by this point disbanded Ceoltóirí Chualann, having concluded that he had taken ensemble playing as far as he could. According to his son Peadar:

> *He decided though, after trying various experiments even with classical music played and arranged for this traditional group ... that there was no further advantage in continuing along this route, as traditional music is a music of the individual.*

He had worked with solo musicians for a while in 1968/69 and he continued his involvement with the choir. His funeral in Cúil Aodha was a testimony to the respect in which he was held throughout the country. Thousands poured into the little village of Cúil Aodha, far too many to be accommodated in the church. There was a general feeling, especially amongst young people, that something more than his life had ended with his death.

Ó RIADA'S LEGACY

There is no doubt that Ó Riada's contribution to Irish music enriched and renewed it. By the time he died it was in a healthier state than it had been for many years. His achievements were many, not least among them being the raised status traditional music now enjoyed. He also demonstrated to young people that there was in Irish music an energy and spirit that equalled anything popular contemporary music had to offer. His great respect and love for traditional music did not make him a conservative, although he well understood that conservatism had kept the tradition alive: 'You might compare the progress of tradition in Ireland to the flow of a river', he wrote. 'Foreign bodies may fall in, or be dropped in, or thrown in, but they do not divert the course of

He worked at traditional music at all levels and was able to attract an audience for all that kind of music right through the whole perspective of Irish music.[10]

the river, nor do they stop it flowing; it absorbs them, carrying them with it as it flows onwards. Our innate conservatism is responsible for this.'[11]

Through his work with Ceoltóirí Chualann, his film scores, his playing and compositions, he demonstrated the myriad possibilities of Irish music.

His ensemble model was taken up and used as the prototype Irish traditional band, as was his style of arranging. Groups sprang up during the late sixties as a consequence of Ó Riada's leading the way. Some of the best young Irish bands working with traditional and folk material freely experimented (too freely some thought) with the music and with arrangements. Planxty, The Bothy Band, De Danann, Horslips, Moving Hearts, and many others owed a debt to Sean Ó Riada. These bands (of which more is written in Chapters 9 and 10) introduced Irish music to a wider international audience as well as a young Irish audience. Very often listeners and players who were influenced by these bands were drawn back to the root of the tradition, and 'straight' traditional music benefited from this interest. It is remarkable, for instance, the number of young Americans, often with no Irish connections, who have fallen in love with Irish traditional music. They achieve standards of excellence which equal those of native players.

The folk and traditional festivals of the seventies were attended by large numbers of mainland Europeans who had come to learn traditional music. Ireland remained one of the few countries left in Europe whose traditional music was still healthy and popular. Continental European folk and traditional cultures had been eroded by two world wars, fascism, and industrialisation. Meanwhile Ireland's traditional music was moving on into the late twentieth century under full steam. Sean Ó Riada remains one of its guiding spirits.

His spirit lives on in Cúil Aodha. His son Peadar who, like his father, studied music at UCC, lives and works as a musician and composer in the old family house. Under his direction the choir sings at Sunday mass, and they undertake occasional concerts. They sing the Ó Riada masses or Peadar's music: 'It isn't mine, it doesn't come from me, it comes from whatever is behind me – the culture in other words.'

Ó Riada's friend, the poet Tom Kinsella, said of him: 'He reached out and swiftly captured a national audience, lifted the level of musical practice and appreciation, restored to his people an entire cultural dimension, and added no little to the gaiety of the nation.'[12]

11 Seán Ó Riada, *Our Musical Heritage*, p. 20

12 Ibid., p. 12

HOME BOYS HOME

In order to pay the rent we did midnight folk concerts; they were about the only thing we knew, and we had invited our friends who had told us we were folk singers. We didn't know we were folk singers, we were just singing all Irish songs. They liked them.[1]

TOM CLANCY

FOLK AND TRADITIONAL INFLUENCES IN THE SIXTIES

In the sixties in Ireland there was an explosion of music. Seán Ó Riada was revitalising traditional music and introducing it to a new audience. Meanwhile in America and Britain in the late fifties a small but very active folk music movement had been centred around clubs, and progressive social movements. The Weavers, Woody Guthrie, Leadbelly, Oscar Brand, in America, and Ewan MacColl in Britain made folk song relevant to urban audiences.

On St Patrick's Day in 1956, three brothers from Carrick on

1 Tom Clancy. Interview,

BIABH

Suir, Co. Tipperary, found themselves giving their first public concert of Irish folk songs in New York City. With their fourth member, Tommy Makem, the Clancy Brothers became a popular folk group in America, gaining much professional experience there. At their homecoming concerts, where they re-introduced popular folk song to the Irish public, they were hailed as conquering heroes. But it was Irish folk song strongly influenced by the Clancys' American experiences, in a form that had not been heard before in Ireland. The Clancys were ambassadors of folk music which was finding its place in the most highly developed urban society in the world. The music was rooted in an old, mainly rural tradition, but its contemporary expression would from now on be largely urban. Its traditional expression would also find a place in the new world of the twentieth century.

AMERICAN FOLK

Radio and gramophone recordings changed American folk and traditional music, gradually modifying the material from its original 'raw' state. Increasing use was made of instrumentation to achieve a richer, fuller sound. The use of rhythmic backing and harmonies further enhanced this effect. The music developed further and further away from its roots, and displaced the kind of community or family music-making described by Jean Ritchie in Chapter 2.

Almost at the same time as this was happening, traditional music enthusiasts grew concerned about the need to collect and save the store of American folk song, which was disappearing fast, or being rendered unrecognisable by the recording industry. Pioneers of collecting and recording folk music 'in the field' were the father and son team of John and Alan Lomax. Together they spent over fifty years at a task which yielded up a wealth of American folk song from the old English and Scots-Irish ballads of the Appalachians to the blues and spirituals of the black people of the south.

In Angola Prison, Carolina, John Lomax 'discovered' one of the great black singers of the century, Huddy Ledbetter, better known as Leadbelly. Leadbelly sang in a style originating in the blues music of his childhood. He accompanied himself on guitar, and composed his own songs. With the support of the Lomaxes he became a household name.

Huddy Ledbetter, better
known as Leadbelly

Interest in folk and traditional music had increased after the
Second World War. Folk music societies and groups sprang up,
and the centre of much of this activity was in New York City.
Jean Ritchie came to New York in the forties, from Kentucky,
and found herself in demand as a folk singer, first at parties
then as a concert performer. She was singing the folk songs she
had grown up with, and songs composed by herself in folk
idioms, updated reflections of contemporary America.

FOLK AND PROTEST

Folk music in America was originally the music of poor communities (rural and urban), of immigrants and black slaves. Folk music had always had an association with political and social agitation, and with persecution. The struggles of the American labour movement, the lives of black slaves, and poor farmers, are documented in thousands of folk songs. The blues and spirituals are songs which grew out of systematic social injustice. Woody Guthrie, one of the great contemporary folk-song writers, made common cause between the black victims of social injustice and the white. 'This Land', he sang, 'was made for you and me'.

He was a folk singer who travelled around America, singing his songs, not on concert platforms, but in small towns and farms, wherever he could get an audience. In the thirties he hosted a radio show which popularised songs like 'If You Aint Got the Doh-Re-Mi' and 'This Land Is My Land'. Using the melodic structures of existing folk tunes, Woody wrote songs which reflected the reality of life in America around him. The thirties was a time when small farmers displaced from the Oklahoma Dust Bowl were forced to work for slave wages on Californian fruit farms. It was a time when the hobo rode the freight trains, and was a familiar but marginalised figure in

Woody Guthrie

American society. Woody knew what he was singing about. He had been a hobo himself and had endured poverty in the Midwest farm lands. In the rich state of California he had seen poor migrants turned away at the state line and prevented from entering.

Woody Guthrie and Leadbelly were part of a folk music movement that had also a social and political programme. With people like Pete Seeger they saw folk song as having the capacity to galvanise groups around issues like civil rights, job discrimination, housing, and education. In the witch hunt atmosphere of America in the fifties these were not popular positions. The entertainment industry came in for the particular scrutiny of 'commie' hunters. Folk singer Pete Seeger came under suspicion and was blacked.

NEW FOLK

Pete had travelled the States for some years with Woody Guthrie, learning and singing songs. A member of the Weavers folk group in the fifties, he became a well-known figure on the concert stage, and later on television. With the Weavers he popularised the songs of Woody Guthrie and Leadbelly, as well as his own. Songs like 'Turn, Turn', 'We shall Overcome', 'Where have All the Flowers Gone', and 'Kisses Sweeter than Wine' were all popular favourites, and have been covered by many artists. Pete believes that a good folk melody should be used more than once. 'Kisses Sweeter than Wine' is a good example of an old song revitalised. The melody is that of an Irish song called 'Droimeann Donn Dílis', about a cow, taken to be an allegorical reference to Ireland. 'Droimeann Donn Dílis' became a comic song 'Poor Drimmer' in America, and a version of it was learned by Leadbelly in the thirties. Leadbelly changed the rhythm to suit his style of singing, and as Pete remembers he 'massacred the words too'.

Pete liked the melody, and with Lee Havers of the Weavers put together his new version, 'Kisses Sweeter than Wine'. This was a hit in the fifties and has been covered many times since. The song sports a very mixed pedigree: 'The tune originally came from Ireland. The rhythm came from Africa, and the words from a fellow in Arkansas who met a person from New England in New York City, and was told by a commercial agent "we gotta get a new song to record".'[2]

2 Pete Seeger, Interview.

BIABH

The Clancy Brothers and
Tommy Makem. Success
in America made them
stars in Ireland

THE CLANCYS IN AMERICA

It was in 1947 that Pat and Tom Clancy were forced by
economic depression to leave Ireland. They went first to
Canada, then to the United States. They were interested in
theatre, and, on their arrival in New York in 1950, began
staging plays at the Cherry Lane Theatre in Greenwich Village,
at that time the bohemian centre of the city. It was a hang out
for artists of all kinds. There were coffee shops, theatres,
studios, and venues where artists met and worked.

But by 1953, they were in difficulties: 'We were doing a play,
The Wise have not Spoken – it was a flop; and we had no money;
we had to pay the rent,' Pat Clancy explained. They put on
midnight concerts for their friends who were all folk singers –
to make money to pay rent on the theatre. They were so
successful that, after the Clancys moved from the Cherry Lane
Theatre, they continued them in another theatre nearby. They
sang themselves, but also engaged well-known folk singers of
the time, like Oscar Brand, Pete Seeger, Jean Ritchie, as well
as blues performers like Sonny Terry and Brownie McGhee,
and the Reverend Gary Davis. Then their younger brother Liam
joined them. Then Tommy Makem from Keady in Co. Armagh,
the son of singer Sarah Makem who had been recorded in 1951
by Jean Ritchie, met Liam, through another music collector,
Diane Hamilton. The two teamed up and eventually Tommy

joined Pat and Tom in New York too, to make up 'The Clancy Brothers and Tommy Makem' folk group.

The Clancys more than anyone else were surprised by this turn of events. They had not set out to be 'folk singers'. They had never heard the term until they went to America. As far as they were concerned 'we were just singing all Irish songs'. All the same they couldn't help but notice what was happening: 'you could see the popularity of folk music was just coming in, in the Village only of course at that time, but you could see because the audience was getting bigger and bigger'.

In 1956 the Clancys decided to record their first album, on a company label set up by Pat. The album was called *Irish Songs of Rebellion* and features songs like 'The Rising of the Moon', 'Kelly the Boy From Killane', and 'The Croppy Boy', all well known if not hackneyed songs in Ireland. This was followed shortly by another album of drinking songs called *Come Fill Your Glass with Us*. They had no idea what their move would be, but by now the folk bandwagon was well under way. Tommy Makem remembers: 'Here we were with this vast repertoire of songs that most of the folk singers and folk people had not heard in this country, and none of the songs were learned from books, or from recordings; they were all from the oral tradition we had.'

The Clancys adapted these songs for the American folk audience. They did this by incorporating choral singing and the instrumental accompaniment of guitars and banjo. By doing this they Americanised their Irish repertoire. Guitars and harmony were not native to the Irish tradition. This came because, as Tommy Makem says:

> *We ... saw people like the Weavers. I know I was extremely impressed when I arrived and saw them. Here they were doing songs, the same kind of songs I had known from home. There were four of them singing and they had a guitar and a banjo and it was wonderful music. I began thinking 'My God wouldn't that be tremendous to sing some of our songs like that' and we started doing them and just singing out lustily as well you could.*[3]

For Tommy, Pete Seeger who played with the Weavers, was the main influence: 'The man was magical. I watched him on stage playing his banjo and the electricity just emanated out of him. He could get up and play his banjo and the entire

3 Tommy Makem.
Interview, *BIABH*

audience were all involved in everything he was doing.... He certainly influenced me very strongly and hundreds more like me – thousands I'd say.'

Tommy introduced the five-string banjo into Irish folk music. The five-string banjo is a product of America's mixed racial history. A long-necked instrument with a gourd sound-box was thought to have come first from West Africa to the Caribbean, and from there to America with the first black slaves. In seventeenth-century plantation America it was known as the 'banjar'. It originally had four strings, but a fifth short octave string was added in the early nineteenth century. Allegedly responsible for this addition was an Irish American musician called Joe Sweeny. The fifth string is used like a drone, to sound a continuous note, not unlike the effect of the drone in Irish traditional piping. Frets were added later on, and wire strings were introduced in addition to gut. The banjo was used extensively in minstrel shows and in time became a respectable parlour instrument. The tenor or short-necked, four-string, steel-strung banjo eventually took over from the Appalachian long-necked five-string banjo. This instrument

Tommy Makem playing Irish music in New York, on an Appalachian 5-string banjo

became popular in Ireland in the twentieth century and, with the banjo-mandolin, was used in céilí bands from the thirties, playing traditional music. In America the five-string was rehabilitated by Pete Seeger and Earl Scruggs in the forties and fifties.

In introducing a five-string Appalachian banjo to the Clancy Brothers' instrumentation, Tommy Makem enhanced further the 'American' effect of the repertoire.

> *The Irish in America never came to see our shows.... They were used to 'Danny Boy', 'When Irish Eyes are Smiling', the clichéed Irish American songs, what they considered the Irish songs. When we started singing things like 'Brennan on the Moor' and 'Will Ye Go Lassie Go' and 'The Jug of Punch' they didn't think they were Irish songs at all, in fact a few people who came to the Blue Angel shouted up at the end of the show, 'When are you going to sing an Irish song?' They didn't recognise these as being Irish.*[4]

By the fifties, much of the Irish-American community had settled in the suburbs. Irish traditional music enjoyed no great popularity with Irish-Americans. Traditional music was found in little enclaves of native-born Irish immigrants in Chicago, Boston, New York, and cities of the east coast. The Clancy brothers and Tommy Makem had little contact with any of these communities. They circulated in an artistic milieu based in Greenwich Village which was regarded with suspicion (if it was known about at all) by middle America, and that included Irish-America. Of second-, third- and older-generation Irish-Americans Mick Moloney has written that they had gravitated over the years 'towards a body of nostalgic sentimental song that painted a rosy, romantic scenario of a little green haven nestling in a corner of paradise'.

This, he explains, was a consequence of rejecting traditional music 'that was associated with a low-status, poverty stricken peasant environment'.[5]

Irish-Americans as a group were socially conservative. The beatniks of Greenwich Village, and the politics of the folk movement were enough to put them off the Clancy Brothers.

As far as 'traditional' Irish-America went, the Clancys were not traditional musicans. According to Ciarán Mac Mathúna who had recorded Irish immigrant musicians in America: 'to a certain extent maybe the traditional Irish musician wouldn't

4 Pat Clancy. Interview, *BIABH*

5 Mick Moloney, *Irish Ethnic Recordings*, p. 85

have fully approved of what the Clancys were doing, and they still argue about this today'.

This situation changed completely when the Clancys were suddenly catapulted to fame in 1961. The Clancys were then playing in the Blue Angel, the biggest nightclub in New York, which was a popular haunt of talent scouts. The scout for *The Ed Sullivan Show* saw them and booked them. This was then the most popular show on American TV. It had an audience of 80 million viewers and went out live on Sunday nights from eight to nine o'clock. The Clancys went on and, as luck would have it, ended up performing for eighteen minutes when the star act failed to appear. Endorsed by Ed Sullivan they were delivered into the hands of Irish-America, wherein they received a rapturous reception.

This was the turning point. 'It wasn't until we got the blessing of *The Ed Sullivan Show*', says Liam, 'that we were considered to be legitimate Irishmen'. After this appearance their career as a professional folk group was launched. 'They were', says Mick Moloney, 'the first Irish-born entertainers since John McCormack to achieve international recognition'.

We were booked into the Gate of Horn Club in Chicago the week [after the Ed Sullivan Show] and we went there on the Monday ... Tom and I were walking down the street with the Aran sweaters around our necks (now we weren't known in Chicago, we had never been there). Some guy shouted 'Hi fellas, you were great last night' ... Tom turned to me and said 'Hey we're ... famous!' [6]

HOME FOR A WHILE IN THE OLD COUNTRY

In 1962 Ciarán Mac Mathúna was in America recording Irish traditional musicians for Radio Eireann, the state broadcasting service. The musicians he found were playing in small Irish communities, in each other's houses and at competitions organised by Comhaltas Ceoltóirí Eireann, a recently founded musical organisation set up to revive the playing of traditional music. Tommy Makem remembers Ciarán telling him that in every home he visited: 'he saw record jackets with these four fellas with white sweaters on them ... so he took a couple back home. He started to play them on Radio Eireann. Some of the other fellas in Radio Eireann ... started to play them and ... songs like "The Holy Ground" just went sky high.'

6 Liam Clancy. Interview, *BIABH*

The Clancy Brothers' insignia were white (bánín) Aran sweaters. Their lusty delivery, whistles, whoops, thigh-slapping and repertoire of folk songs attracted the Irish audience as no other act had done. Any child growing up in Ireland in the sixties knew at least one Clancy brothers' song. One of the most popular was 'The Holy Ground' which was ironically a seafaring song said to be about a district known as the 'Holy Ground' in Cobh, formerly Queenstown, Co. Cork. This was the port from which hundreds of thousands of Irish emigrants embarked for America.

Ciarán had been present at a Clancy Brothers' concert in Carnegie Hall and had been impressed by the huge crowd of about three thousand which had attended. He introduced himself to the Clancys and suggested they come to Ireland to do some concerts. Although initially apprehensive at the prospect, they agreed: 'We were nervous of it. I mean it was alright to get up in a strange place and sing something like "O'Donnell Abu", but as far as we were concerned every child in Ireland knew "O'Donnell Abu" and we wouldn't have the neck to get up and sing it in Ireland.'[7]

Their first Irish tour, and subsequent tours, sold out and the Clancys were greeted as superstars everywhere they went. Their albums were in most Irish homes. They went into the repertoire of Irish singers, amateur and professional. Part of the attraction of the songs was the lively way they were presented. They were easy to sing and they were Irish, or considered to be Irish. Seán Ó Riada had shown that it was possible to make of Irish traditional music valid cultural expression in an urban Ireland. The Clancys did the same for folk songs. Moreover, as Ciarán Mac Mathúna points out: 'a very much wider audience than Irish music ever had before, went back then to hear the real tradition; they discovered the original thing; they were led back. . . . to the source of these songs . . . by the Clancy Brothers and it also brought them back to instrumental music'.

The Clancy format was universally copied. 'Ballad groups' proliferated, as did the phenomena known as 'singing pubs', offering their own brand of Clancy pastiche. Many of these groups and venues were cheap imitations of the real thing, and by the end of the decade the golden goose that was the ballad boom had been all but strangled. Singers of this type were getting a bad press, and fewer gigs. Then the scene moved on.

But the Clancys had played a very important part in starting a revival which had far-reaching consequences for the future. 'Somebody wrote about Moore's Melodies . . . that Mr Moore

Fare thee well my darling Dinah, A thousand times adieu, For we're going away from the Holy Ground, And the girls we all love true. We'll sail the salt sea over And we'll return to shore, To see again the girls we love And the Holy Ground once more. Fine Girl You Are![8]

7 Pat Clancy. Interview, *BIABH*

8 From 'The Holy Ground'

had taken the wild harp of Eireann and turned it into a musical snuff box. Well the Clancys took it out of the snuff box and put it into a pint glass ... that had more guts and less sentiment.'[9]

> *Ireland went downhill in the 1940s and fifties. There was huge desolate emigration in the fifties. The Clancy Brothers came back wearing, on the front of their records, dress suits. They were coming out of Carnegie Hall with dress suits and an Aran jersey over their arm. It was terrific, you know. The Irish had arrived in some way. It also coincided with John Kennedy being made President, the first Catholic person to become President ... the energy they got in the new world – that New World energy – came back to Ireland and resuscitated people in Ireland as well.*[10]

The Clancys had to endure a certain amount of criticism about playing fast and loose with the traditional. This did not bother them unduly. As Pat Clancy sees it:

> *There was always this thing: 'are you destroying Irish folk music?' ... what we did with the songs is what's been done over generations, you adapt them to your own. The folk singers who picked them up in the cottages and the fields – they changed them to suit themselves ... we weren't answerable to anybody, in fact we were out making a living at something we love doing, and we never had to answer, and never will answer to anybody for it.*

BOB DYLAN AND THE CLANCYS

By the 1960s the folk revival in America had attracted the popular support of a large young audience. Many factors coincided to produce an extraordinary outpouring of traditional and folk-influenced material, as well as recordings and performances of 'straight' traditional music.

Greenwich Village in New York city remained the focal point of much of it. And clubs and coffee houses were popular venues for folk music of all kinds, especially on college campuses. In loosely organised folk sessions it was possible for anyone present to get up and sing; to perform their own or traditional material.

Straight blues and traditional music, and the contemporary folk-song genre were blossoming. Under the sway of Guthrie and Seeger, young singer-songwriters were producing songs

9 Ciarán Mac Mathúna, Interview, *BIABH*

10 David Hammond, Interview, *BIABH*

about the human condition in urban America. Bob Dylan was the archetype, having left his home in Hibbing for Greenwich Village, and a career as a travelling singer in the Guthrie mode.

Dylan frequented clubs and coffee houses in the Village where the Clancys performed, and today acknowledges the influence of Liam Clancy on his ballad style. Dylan's most famous borrowing from the Clancys was the melody from an Irish song 'The Patriot Game' written by the Irish songwriter Dominic Behan, brother of Brendan Behan the writer. The melody is originally American. It appears in an Appalachian song 'The Nightingale'. 'The Patriot Game' recounts the tale of one O'Hanlon, an IRA volunteer. To this melody Dylan set the savage lyrics of 'With God on our Side', his indictment of American, so-called Christian values. This song featured on the Neville Brothers' album *Yellow Moon* released in 1989. Another case of a good folk melody never losing its relevance.

For a long time Dylan immersed himself in the idioms and conventions of folk music. He and Joan Baez, another young folk singer from Boston, were the king and queen of the sixties' folk. Dylan and the folk world were unprepared for the adulation he received. Dylan's music and Dylan himself stood for a new set of values, more honest, and less materialistic, than those of the previous generation. These values reflected the growing opposition to America's involvement in Vietnam, support for the civil rights movement led by Dr Martin Luther King and sexual freedom. Folk music was played on the streets, in parks, and coffee houses. Folk festivals like that of Newport, which had begun in the fifties, featured traditional acts like Jean Ritchie, and Irish 'Sean Nós' singer Joe Heaney, alongside the Clancy Brothers and Bob Dylan. In 1965 when Dylan 'went electric' many folk fans felt betrayed. In fact he brought much of what he'd learned from folk music with him, but from now on rock was to be the dominant element in his music.

It seemed in any event to be a matter of supreme indifference to Dylan, who shrugged off the critics and analysts. 'It's all music,' he said, 'nothing more, nothing less.'

CONTINUING THAT TRADITION

Dylan left folk behind, but others found the traditional source again. Some musicians and singers looked to the native American tradition. Some looked outside America to the Irish tradition.

In New York of course, you had a nice little view of the music, but then all of a sudden I saw my counterparts in Ireland play the tunes and it was amazing; it really spurred me on to try harder to get more tunes and get a better style of playing.... After a while you saw the competitions as less important and just the overall crack of playing tunes together was the most important thing.

EILEEN IVERS[11]

(Opposite top)
Eileen Ivers. An Irish American traditional musician

(Opposite below)
Cherish the Ladies, an all woman group of Irish American traditional musicians and dancers

(Left to right) Robbie O'Connell, Mick Moloney and Jimmy Keane recording for *Bringing It All Back Home* in New York

11 Eileen Ivers. Interview,

BIABH

Particularly amongst the young Irish-American generation the revival of interest in folk music encouraged them to play. Comhaltas Ceoltóirí Eireann (in English, The Musicians Association of Ireland) had been set up in the fifties to promote the playing of Irish traditional music.

Branches were set up in the States and 'Fleadhanna Cheoil' (competitions) were organised to give American players a focus for their activities. The work of Comhaltas was assisted, both in Ireland and America, by the folk boom led by the Clancys, and the innovative work done by Seán Ó Riada in traditional music. A lively healthy traditional music developed as a result.

Nor did Irish traditional music enthusiasts in America have to travel to Ireland to hear the real thing. There were enough traditional players in America to pass the tradition on to the next generation.

Mick Moloney, Robbie O'Connell, and Jimmy Keane recorded a selection of tunes known as 'Reevy's' for *Bringing It All Back Home*. They are named after the musician who composed them, Irish-born Ed Reevy who died in America in 1989. Mick Moloney considers Reevy to be 'one of the greatest composers of Irish music this century ... and certainly the most prolific'. He was born in 1899 in County Cavan and went to America when he was a boy. He was an accomplished fiddle player, but also a composer of tunes in the traditional idiom. He did not make a professional career of traditional music but played constantly, particularly in the hey-day of the music in America, in the twenties and thirties. He turned to composition in the forties, and his tunes travelled back to Ireland in the hands of

returning musicians. From here they went into the repertoire of players who were often unaware that their composer was alive and living in America. Mick Moloney remembers learning 'Reevy tunes' in the sixties in Ireland and making the assumption that they had always been there.

> *Suddenly in Ed Reevy's own lifetime his music composed here in Philadelphia had become part of the repository of traditional music, carrying on a great tradition of composing and assimilation of the dance music in the culture.... It's an amazing story of how music composed here in this country should go back to the home country and influence that culture itself.*

Mick Moloney, who works as a musician, music teacher and academic in the States, has identified three types of traditional players in America. These are first the native-born Irish, secondly Americans who have no connection with Ireland, and thirdly young Irish-Americans, often the children or grandchildren of Irish immigrants. This last group is by far the largest. In New York, *Bringing It All Back Home* recorded a group of young Irish-American traditional players. They call themselves 'Cherish the Ladies', the name of a well-known jig tune, because they're an all-woman group.

Eileen Ivers is a fiddle player with Cherish the Ladies and has a background typical of other band members. Eileen's parents are both Irish-born, and Eileen grew up in New York in an Irish neighbourhood in the Bronx. She was taught the fiddle by a famous traditional player and teacher, Martin Mulvihill. He ran a school in the Bronx where other Irish-American kids learned to play. The competitive side to playing is important in America and children are encouraged to compete. Eileen feels that this was necessary in her case. Winners in the American Fleadhanna go on to Ireland to compete in the Fleadhanna there, the ultimate prize being an 'All Ireland' trophy. Eileen was very impressed by her first experience of an Irish Fleadh.

Eileen is now twenty-five and has won the All Ireland Fiddle Championship seven times. She has won the All Ireland Senior Fiddle Championship once, the third American ever to do so.

She is a solo performer who moves easily from playing electric fiddle with Irish rock musician Luka Bloom, to traditional music with Cherish the Ladies. She now accompanies her own pupils to Ireland for the Fleadh Cheoil, and the tradition looks

The Furey Brothers
Finbar (pipes) and Eddie
(guitar) play at a Fleadh
Cheoil in the sixties

set to continue for some time yet. Schools like the one Eileen attended in the Bronx play an important part in the transmission of traditional music. The breakdown of the old Irish city neighbourhoods and customs such as house dances brought other systems into being. Oral transmission is still central to the passing on of the tradition though. Players learn from other players, and classes are just one element of the process. Tunes are learned also from records and passed on by cassette tape-recordings. According to Mick Moloney: 'The cassette recorder has revolutionised the process of acquiring repertoire and styles ... more than any other technological phenomenon.... One consequence has been that the average Irish musician now has a repertoire that older musicians consider massive.'[12]

This new generation of traditional players in America can and do visit Ireland frequently, unlike earlier emigrants. Unfortunately their numbers in America are constantly being swelled by young Irish emigrants newly arrived. Once again the young population of Ireland is being depleted by massive emigration. It may be the case that the future of the tradition will again be entrusted to the players of Irish music in America.

12 Mick Moloney, *Irish
Ethnic Recordings*

CHAPTER NINE

MOVING ON

We had this idea of Ireland rammed down our throats. So we threw it up.[1]

BONO OF U2

THE ROCKING OF IRISH MUSIC

The tide of change was in full spate in Ireland in the sixties. Movement away from the land into towns and cities intensified and the pace of industrialisation accelerated. Standards of living rose and the working week was shortened.

Free post-primary education was introduced in 1964 and life changed for the new generation of young Irish. Those whose parents did not have the means to pay for post-primary education were now able to continue their schooling. Relieved of the necessity of working, they were free to join the youth culture and become consumers in that culture.

It soon became evident that many young people rejected the Irish stereotypes presented as role models by official institutions of culture, education and religion. British radio and television stations, American programmes and the recording industry were establishing new cultural norms. These were secular, individualistic and materialistic. American and English popular music held out exciting prospects of cultural redefinition. Rock 'n' roll, rhythm and blues, and the blues arrived in Ireland. Things would never be the same again.

This music espoused a world view of personal freedom. What were perceived as irrelevant and outmoded restrictions on

1 Bono of U2. Interview, *BIABH*

sexual behaviour and personal expression were dismissed. It questioned authority. It was embraced in Ireland by the young, the bored and the angry.

Mainstream Irish music of the time was the music of ballad groups modelled on the Clancy Brothers, and the music of the 'show bands'. Ballad singing generally took place in pubs and concert halls and was usually a sing-along type of family entertainment. 'Ballad session' radio and television programmes were also popular. Most families' record collections boasted a couple of ballad albums.

Show bands were primarily dance bands. Dance halls were the social centres for young Irish adults in the sixties. Irish dance halls frequently accommodated two and three thousand people and many show bands worked every night of the week. Show bands played no original material. The line-up was usually seven to ten musicians comprising guitars, bass, drums, vocals and a brass section. Show band musicians were always neatly dressed and all wore the same type of suit. Dances turned in a huge profit and offered lucrative work to musicians working in the bigger bands. Show bands operated a monopoly in this system. Their venues were not open to groups performing other material. Music like rock 'n' roll, r'n'b or blues were excluded. The system also forced good musicians to work in show bands when their musical preferences lay elsewhere. Things gradually changed. Clubs opened in the cities to cater for different kinds of music. Universities and colleges around the country also provided venues for fledgling bands and provided alternatives to ballad groups and show bands.

ONE FOR THE MONEY, TWO FOR THE SHOW

Musician Paul Brady's early enthusiasms were for Elvis Presley, Chuck Berry, Jerry Lee Lewis, and Little Richard. He played the piano and and greatly admired American rock 'n' roll piano-players.

Coinciding with his initiation into rock 'n' roll, the Clancy Brothers were storming through Ireland. He remembers not being 'musically disposed to that kind of thing' but being drawn in by their energy and success despite himself. He never saw the Clancy Brothers' phenomenon as part of a 'folk movement' though, 'this was still popular culture in Ireland ... it was just around'.

This was a common feeling amongst young people. Folk songs and ballads were 'just around' and not an exciting or interesting genre in themselves. Many young people who attended school in the sixties and early seventies shared the experience of Bono and Philip Chevron who use the same expression to describe their experience of the Clancy Brothers: they were 'rammed down our throats'.

The ballad-group format was generally harmony singing, accompanied by indifferent guitar playing. There was no emphasis on instrumental playing and no attempt to include instrumental numbers in the repertoire. The energy and drive that characterised the Clancy Brothers was not really equalled by the copy-cat groups who tended to cover the same material. The seam was exhausted by the late sixties, and ballad groups in this mode were on the way out.

During the sixties Seán Ó Riada had revived interest in the instrumental tradition, and explored new ways of playing the old music. Meanwhile American and English bands like the Byrds, The Lovin' Spoonful, the Stones, and musicians like Eric Clapton and Bob Dylan incorporated elements of traditional music in their performance. The black tradition of blues singing and instrumentation, white folk song, and old time country music was surfacing in popular music. Mixed up in the cocktail of rock 'n' roll it arrived in Ireland, and met an indigenous music culture of traditional music and ballad singing.

Because Ireland was a small country with a population of less than three million people, there was no great degree of specialisation in the beginning. Musicians simply took whatever they liked from the music on offer, and this eclecticism produced some exotic results. Many musicians who played in the pubs and clubs around Dublin and elsewhere eventually wound up playing with all the other musicians on the scene. Thus, you had blues players mixing with traditional, folk, rock, and contemporary players.

Alec Finn, a member of the traditionally based group, De Danann, came to live in Dublin in the sixties. His main interest then was in the blues; he shared a flat with rock musician Phil Lynott; and he listened to traditional and rock music. 'It didn't matter,' he says of that time, 'whether you were a traditional musician or a rock musician. They all sort of drank in the same bars to a great extent and had jams together and what have you. Everyone blended in very well together.'

The pub has a special significance in Irish cultural life. It was and is associated with the playing of music. It provided Alec with his first introduction to Irish traditional music:

I suppose the first thing that really caught my attention would have been, you know, rock 'n' roll – everybody's first big exciting thing was rock 'n' roll, and it was for me too: it was no different.

PAUL BRADY[2]

2 Paul Brady. Interview.

BIABH

> *In England when I used to play country blues, we used to look for sessions in pubs ... although we were looked on as being a bit peculiar for doing so. But I found it amazing when I came to Ireland that people just went into pubs, that virtually didn't know each other, that played the same kind of music and could sit down and have all this amazing interaction ... that was the most amazing thing about it ... I don't think it exists anywhere else in the world.*

The pub was the place where many Irish musicians learned to play, where they met other musicians, and heard other kinds of music. A music that was rock-inspired but Irish in character grew out of this interaction.

CELTIC ROCK

Barry Devlin, Jim Lockhart, Eamonn Carr, Charles O'Connor, and Johnny Fean were young men about Dublin town in the late sixties. The band they formed, Horslips, was to become one of the most influential and popular Irish rock bands of the seventies, and gave birth to a new phenomenon ... Celtic Rock. Horslips performed a mix of country, traditional and folk rock, which was entirely consistent with the music they were hearing in the clubs and pubs around Dublin at the time. The psychedelia-powered hippy culture of the time spawned an interest in the ancient myths and legends of Celtic Ireland. This was an important visual and conceptual element in the band's presentation.

Horslips were middle class and college educated. They worked in advertising and they were fashion conscious; they knew the value of marketing and image making, and they used these skills in presenting the band to the Irish public. This was a novelty at the time. More importantly they knew that many young people in Ireland could not identify with the official view of Irish culture as presented by the Irish tourist board, Irish radio, Irish schools, and so on.

On the other hand Horslips included members whose knowledge of Irish ranged from fluent to fair, and who were interested in, and players of Irish traditional music. They were committed to bringing an Irish cultural dimension to the raw material of electric rock. Horslips was not to be simply a clone of English or American rock bands. They wanted a sound and

Horslips – the originators of Celtic rock in the seventies

material that was clearly Irish but also contemporary popular music. As Jim Lockhart describes it: 'It was a matter of trying to hold out for a more integrated culture as opposed to something second-hand ... which meant forging a new idiom....: It was an attempt to create something indigenous and new, but essentially indigenous.'

Horslips' mixture of acoustic and rock interpretations of Irish instrumental music was instantly attractive. Their clothes and appearance reinforced the Celtic hippy theme. Their stage show incorporated coloured back projections and Celtic set designs. The combination of rock music and theatre was a timely innovation. Noted for musical and literary accomplishment, the Irish have not equalled this with visual sensitivity. Horslips did lead the way in raising the standards of this aspect of presentation.

In March 1972 we played Foxrock Youth Club, in April we played the Stadium and could have filled it twice and by June nobody in Dublin would talk to us.
BARRY DEVLIN
ABOUT
HORSLIPS[3]

Philip Chevron, song writer and member of The Pogues, recording 'Thousands Are Sailing' for *Bringing It All Back Home*, with traditional fiddlers Maíre Breathnach, and Seamus and Kevin Glackin

3 Barry Devlin, *Hot Press*, Vol. 2, No. 16, 25 Jan. 1979

4 Philip Chevron, *Hot Press*, Vol. 12, No. 6, 7 Apr. 1988

In 1972 they recorded their first album. With typical flair they used the Rolling Stones' mobile recording studio, and the album *Horslips – Happy to Meet Sorry to Part* came out on their own label. The thirteen tracks included traditional dance tunes and songs, two of which were in Irish. The range of instruments included electric and acoustic guitars and fiddles, bodhrán, keyboards, flute, mandolin, and concertina. The record was an instant success and was hailed as a breakthrough. Celtic Rock had been born. Their concerts were thronged with young Irish people enamoured by the all-embracing cultural hybrid produced by the band. (Horslips even managed to break the show band stranglehold of the dance halls.) Singles released subsequently, principally 'Dearg Donn' and 'King of the Fairies', classic Celtic rockers, raced to the top of the charts and stayed there.

From 1972 until their demise in 1980 Horslips recorded ten albums. They wrote their own material and used Irish dance tunes, old harp music, airs and marches, songs in Irish and English, and folk music of other cultures. Throughout the seventies they toured extensively in Ireland, Europe and the States. They achieved cult status in parts of America, were briefly popular in Britain during the folk rock era, but never succeeded in breaking into the international rock world. Celtic rock was not yet capable of translation into the international language of rock.

At home in Ireland the purists were horrified, the critics dismissive, and young audiences wildly approving. Horslips had set out to provide an indigenous rock idiom and for a while they achieved this. Philip Chevron, now a member of The Pogues, remembers growing up in Dublin in the sixties hating ballads and Irish music generally and then being struck by the Horslips' thunderbolt: 'Irish music as officially presented didn't speak for me or for thousands upon thousands like me. But Horslips did and some Horslips fans then went away and listened to Seán Ó Riada records.'[4] Chevron himself was one of those drawn by the tradition that inspired the band.

The Celtic rock craze spawned a few bands in the Horslips' mode, like Spud and Mushroom, but none matched the ingenuity or style of the prototype. This phase in Irish music history ended with the last Horslips' gigs in 1980. The Horslips' real successors are musicians like Philip Chevron who do not copy what Horslips did, but take the idea that Irish traditional music belongs to everybody, and put it into practice. This is Horslips' considerable achievement.

WHISKEY IN THE JAR/IRISH ROCK

In March 1973, a couple of months after Horslips released their first album, an Irish single went into the English charts and reached number six. The singer was Phil Lynott, an Irishman born in England of an Irish mother and Brazilian father. The band was Thin Lizzy. The single was a well-known Irish ballad, 'Whiskey in the Jar', a hearty song of a highwayman betrayed by his sweetheart, with a rousing chorus:

Phil Lynott (centre) with Thin Lizzy. He brought an Irish sensibility to rock music in the seventies

> *Whack fol de daddy o*
> *Whack fol de daddy o*
> *There's whiskey in the jar.*

Thin Lizzy had recorded the song more in the way of a joke than anything else. Phil Lynott was a singer and song writer heavily influenced by Jimi Hendrix and progressive rock music of the day. He had also spent time with the folkies and blues players around Dublin and was attracted by the lyrical element in the folk repertoire. The record company felt that 'Whiskey in the Jar' originally destined to be a B side on the new Lizzy single, would make a better A side. This opinion proved correct. The song was also a runaway success in Ireland where it

I had an album of Dolly McMahon's with the uilleann pipes and all that stuff. I liked it too.
VAN MORRISON[5]

received continuous airplay. Right from the start its opening electric guitar lick set the pace for a loud rocky, high-energy version of the old Clancy Brothers' staple.

Phil Lynott's song writing was located in the ballad form. His songs were set in contemporary Ireland, particularly in the Dublin of his childhood. His skilful, lyrical evocations of life in sixties and seventies Ireland touched his audience personally. Lyrically he was a romantic and his fans approved. Early in the seventies Thin Lizzy adopted a heavy rock format to harness their loud and energetic output. They gained admission to the American and British progressive rock circuit and achieved the status of superstars in the mid-seventies.

Tragically Phil Lynott's life was cut short at the age of thirty-seven and he is still missed by fans and fellow musicians. His achievement was to bring an Irish sensibility to rock music and put it on the world stage.

CALEDONIAN SOUL/VAN MORRISON

From the beginning, the jazz, blues and gospel influences were mixed in a brew that was inimitably Van Morrison's. In twenty-one years of recording, from the seminal and still classic *Astral Weeks* album, Van Morrison remains one of rock's master musicians. His recording history is too extensive to detail here save to say that his recent recordings have revealed a preoccupation with the Celtic roots of his musical inspiration. He is on record as saying that Celtic music, that is the music of Scotland and Ireland, is 'soul music'. The spirit of this music has animated his work intensely over the past eight or nine years, but was apparent in some of his earlier albums also. Ireland, and the Belfast of his youth, are at the centre of his creative source as evidenced in tracks like 'Madame George' and 'Cypress Avenue' on *Astral Weeks*. The mystical, soul quality of his song-writing arises from his belief in a 'Celtic' consciousness.

In 1973 on *Hardnose the Highway* he recorded a folk song 'Purple Heather'. Coincidentally this had been recorded nearly ten years earlier by the Clancy Brothers. In their repertoire it was popularly known as 'Will Ye Go Lassie Go'. It's a Scottish folk song which had been popular in Ireland for many years and Van picked it up in Belfast: 'I heard the McPeakes do it at a party in Belfast a long long time ago. I'd probably heard it from my mother but the McPeakes sold me on it. I thought it was one of the greatest things I'd ever heard. Period. On record or off record.'[6]

5 Van Morrison to Donal Corvan, *Hot Press*, Vol. 1, No. 1, Jun. 1977

6 Ibid.

The McPeakes were a well-known Belfast family with a large repertoire of folk songs. Francey and Francis McPeake, father and son, were also accomplished uilleann pipers. The family had a unique style of harmony singing accompanied by uilleann pipes, not an instrument used for this purpose. In the fifties they were visited by song collectors like Peter Kennedy from BBC radio, and by Pete Seeger who filmed them in Belfast in 1953.

Van's nasal tonality on the vocals of 'Purple Heather' and the extended decorative melody line, produced a result which was both contemporary and true to the spirit of the folk song. In 1980 he devoted much time to studying Celtic culture, in its philosophical and mystical dimensions. In a way this was a reaction to his early exposure to the commercial world of the music-recording industry, of which he was suspicious and about whose motivations he remains cynical. He felt that the industry had turned the art of music into 'an entertainment process; a means not an end, a medium not a message. Music has lost its soul.' His own family background and early playing days had been conducted in the atmosphere of community activity, where music had a meaning, and a 'soul'. His parents were Jehovah's Witnesses. Perhaps the spiritual and religious element, dominant in his performing and writing, stems from here. He perceives that: 'this music that came out of gospel and blues and hillbilly music has developed into something that is rootless ... some of us have to put some of the threads together to make it real – to put some reality into it.'[7]

He admitted in this interview in 1982 that he hadn't really 'rated' Irish music in Belfast when he was young. Now he was returning to the roots. 'I think,' he said: 'it can be dangerous to not validate the music of where you're from, for anybody.... For me it's traditional. I'm a traditionalist. I believe in tracing things back to the source and finding out what the real thing was, and how it changed.'

Beautiful Vision, released in 1982, was the outcome of this first journey back to the Celtic homeland. It integrated folk and rhythm and blues idioms, embracing traditional music in the use uilleann pipes in 'Celtic Ray'. 'Cleaning Windows' is an affectionate hymn to his youth and musical roots in Belfast. The traditional aspect is heightened on the next album *Inarticulate Speech of the Heart*. Here he makes use of uilleann pipes, and acoustic instrumentation on 'Celtic Swing', while the jaunty 'Connswater' seems to derive from the spirit of Irish march music.

7 Van Morrison to Dermot Stokes, *Hot Press*, Vol. 6, No. 6, 1 Apr. 1982

Inarticulate Speech of the Heart was followed in 1985 by *A Sense of Wonder*. Here Van used the Irish trad/rock band The Moving Hearts who contribute one track 'Boffyflow and Spike', and whose piper Davy Spillane plays on the title track.

No Guru, No Method, No Teacher was released in 1986. This time he included two songs on the exile theme: 'One Irish Rover' and 'Got to go Back'.

The culmination of his love affair with Irish music resulted in the *Irish Heartbeat* album, when, as one critic exclaimed: 'Van Morrison has publicly laid his Celtic music cards on the table, making explicit what has long been implicit in his music.' In this album he collaborated with the traditional group The Chieftains. *Irish Heartbeat* is his interpretation of mainly folk material like 'The Star of the County Down', a bouncy Northern song on which Van sings and plays the drums; 'My Lagan Love', a haunting and beautiful modal air which has a difficult melodic progression; and 'On Raglan Road', a song associated with another great Irish singer of ballads, the late Luke Kelly. On the old Belfast street song 'I'll Tell Me Ma', another Clancy Brothers' favourite, Van delivers a lusty performance with Belfast intonation, obviously enjoying himself in the process of rediscovering his Northern persona.

When the album was released he remarked to one interviewer: 'Now you get all these crossovers. People have to make connections because in this modern age we live in, which is the video age, you're allowed five minutes. You have to make more connections than that, otherwise you're gonna starve.'

You tend to put a glass case around folk music but I think U2 are a folk group ... an out and out folk band – we're the loudest folk band you'll ever hear.[8]

UNFORGETTABLE FIRE: U2

Undoubtedly the most important rock band to come out of Ireland and feature on a world stage is U2. Formed in 1976 when the band members were still schoolboys, U2 achieved the dizzy heights of the cover of *Rolling Stone* magazine by 1985. The distinctive U2 style, developed over the years, is loud and raw, characterised by Bono's huge voice and impassioned lyrics, and the guitar sound of The Edge, Dave Evans.

Bono's lyrics range from political and social issues like American imperialism, heroin addiction, human rights violations and war, to more personal songs of love and relationships. The band has been associated for many years with causes like Amnesty International, C N D, and Live Aid.

Musically the band is committed to an exploration of the roots of rock 'n' roll as was evident in their last album *Rattle*

8 Bono. Interview,

BIABH.

and Hum. U2 differs from other aspiring Irish rock bands in that it set its sights on America rather than Britain. Bono drew from American musical and lyrical inspiration. It was after all 'the birthplace of rock 'n' roll'. Out of this involvement with American music Bono discovered his Irish identity. It came as a revelation to him that Irish music had contributed to rock 'n' roll. He sees the ballad as playing a crucial role in that contribution and this is where his notion of Irishness is rooted. The Irish component in his work is 'the tradition of the story-teller that comes across – the Irish tradition of the story-teller'.

As for performance, 'the Irish are less uptight about what's inside them, therefore they let it out easier and it comes out in a raw way and that's very like the spirit of black music and gospel music'.

Bob Dylan has for a long time been an influence. He was surprised to find that: 'Dylan talks about the Clancy Brothers, and the McPeakes and how much he was influenced by Irish

Bono of U2, 'I think there's an Irishness to what U2 do'

music. He sees it as a central and formative influence on his own work. That blew my mind when he told me this because I'd never thought of him in that way.'

Bono had rejected all aspects of Irish music and culture when he was at school: 'I rebelled against being Irish, I rebelled against speaking the Irish language, Irish culture … Batman, Robin, Superman – that was more part of my experience than Finn McCool and the legends and mythology of Ireland.'

Something of Irish culture did manage to penetrate this attitude. One of his teachers introduced him to the music of Seán Ó Riada which, despite himself, he liked. Then in 1973, as I have mentioned, Thin Lizzy had a hit with an old Clancy Brothers' song 'Whiskey in the Jar'. 'In fact I think one of the first things I ever played on acoustic guitar was "Whiskey in the Jar" but that was before the electric version came out.'

Since then he has been on 'a voyage of self-discovery' through Irish music. He now finds himself drawn to 'the pure … poetic spirit of an instrument like the uillean pipes'. At the same time he is grappling with the problem of Irish identity in the late twentieth century: 'The confusion over my own identity and the group's identity is part of the reason why I'm digging into Irish folk music and the ballad form.'

Bono feels that U2 is a rock band which has an indigenous Irish personality: 'I think there's an Irishness to what U2 do; I'm not quite sure what it is. I think it's something to do with the romantic spirit of the words I write, but also of the melodies that Edge makes on the guitar. Now the rock 'n' roll element that comes through Larry would hardly be Irish, yet the abandonment in the way he plays the kit is intrinsically Irish.' This feeling for and exploration of Irish balladry and music will continue to be reflected in his song writing: 'I think … Irish music reminds us of the humanity that we're losing, of a past that we all share. It's a common past and Irish music is a part of it.'

SINÉAD O'CONNOR

In 1982 fourteen-year-old Sinéad O'Connor made her rock music début with a band called In Tua Nua. In Tua Nua was a rock band with Irish acoustic overlays, and Sinéad sang on what was to be that band's first release on the Island label. This was an auspicious start and was followed by a short stint in another band, before being signed to make an album of her own material.

The *Lion and the Cobra* appeared in 1987 when she was nineteen, a prodigious achievement for such a young singer-songwriter. On the strength of its success she became a star, especially fêted in Ireland where her shaved head, and waif-like appearance added to the mystique. To hear her perform her own material is a powerful, emotional experience. Her voice is more than equal to the demands she makes of it.

The *Lion and the Cobra* displays an astonishing vocal mastery and highly developed instincts for production. She has a strong true voice which needs neither accompaniment nor studio effects to show it off. On her most recent album *I do not Want what I cannot Have* (1989) she included a song she had been singing unaccompanied for some time. On the album it is unaccompanied save for a drum backing. 'I am Stretched on your Grave' has lyrics by the Irish poet Frank O'Connor, and music by singer Philip King. The words are a translation of a twelfth-century poem in Irish 'Ta mé sínte ar do thuama' and the air is a composition in the style of the 'Sean Nós', or unaccompanied mode. The song describes the grief of a man for the girl he loved who has died. The emotional intensity which Sinéad O'Connor is able to bring to the performance of this song made it a sound but daring choice for inclusion on a rock album.

While she publicly disavows any idea of Ireland as anything other than a modern twentieth-century society, her choice of material, and singing style belie this. The vocal influences, particularly the emphasis on the solo voice, are Irish and pre-pop. 'I am Stretched on your Grave' is frequently mistaken for 'the real thing', an Irish traditional song. When she was a child, her father, who was a good Irish tenor, taught her Irish songs and ballads to sing. She apparently used to record these into his dictaphone. Nowadays the folk and 'Celtic' elements are still there mixed with rap, funk, and all the other elements that go into contemporary music.

Mainstream rock has come to stay in Ireland. There are big audiences for a variety of contemporary rock from rap to MOR. Some of the best of the Irish bands and musicians working in these idioms have taken inspiration, wittingly or otherwise, from the great store of singing and instrumental music that makes up the Irish tradition. Whether it is in the lyrical spirit, or the performance, or the actual cadences of the music itself, it is there and undeniable. Sinéad O'Connor and Bono exemplify this, as did the bands which went before them. Irish music in this vein has a great future according to Bono.

[Irish music] continues, incorporating percussion, incorporating things like power and distorted guitar, incorporating the synthesiser ... the English language as well as the Irish language. This is the future ... I'm signing up anyway, I'm signing up.[9]

9 Ibid.

CHAPTER TEN

NO FRONTIERS: IRISH MUSIC IN THE SEVENTIES AND EIGHTIES

For me it was the fact that I was being more excited by Irish music than I had been previously by American and British rock 'n' roll.[1]

CHRISTY MOORE

NEW FOLK

The seventies was an exciting decade for Irish traditional and folk music.

It was a time of folk and traditional music festivals, and of small record labels willing to record the musical output of this new generation of Irish bands and musicians. The vibrant music scene was a reflection of the general mood of the country when, for the first time ever, Irish emigrants were returning home to live. And, for the first time too, young Irish people were not forced to leave Ireland to find work. Ireland now boasted the youngest population in Europe and Irish music had a bigger audience than ever before. Music flourished in this atmosphere.

1 Christy Moore. Interview,

BIABH

The decade produced some outstanding bands, and solo artists. Many, but not all of the bands, have since broken up, but most of the musicians are still performing. The creative interaction between diverse musical forms – traditional, folk, blues, country and rock – set contemporary Irish music on its feet.

The eighties saw these explorations, with some exceptions, moving away from acoustic folk and traditional genres. The new music was contemporary, indigenous, and spoke with an Irish accent.

PLANXTY

Although they played traditional material, most of the seventies' bands had few members who came from the 'pure' tradition, i.e. had grown up playing orally transmitted music. This was true of Planxty, one of the most important and innovative bands of this time. Only one of its members, the piper Liam O'Flynn, fell into the category of traditional musician. Like most of the younger Irish generation the rest had grown up listening to rock 'n' roll and pop music. They came to traditional music via the folk revival of the sixties.

The instigator of Planxty (the name comes from a title for a type of seventeenth-century harp tune) was Christy Moore who returned to Ireland in the early seventies, having worked the folk-club circuit there. Andy Irvine and Donal Lunny made up the four.

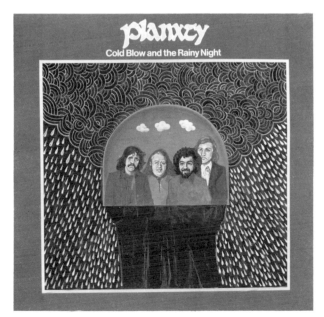

It was mainly a song-based band. Instrumental music featuring the piping of Liam O'Flynn and guitar, bouzouki and mandolin playing made up about a third of the repertoire.

Donal Lunny, who had grown up in Newbridge, Co. Kildare — Christy Moore's home town — had been accidentally drawn into traditional music. Originally attracted to rock 'n' roll, he learned to play guitar. The only opportunity to play was in local pubs where traditional musicians used to meet: There weren't a lot of guitars around so I had a free rein; ... that's where I became properly involved in traditional music. I wasn't really thinking about what I was doing.'

One of the first problems Planxty had to resolve was the accompanying of Irish traditional music. Donal was aware that it was essentially an unaccompanied form, but:

> *I've always had strong feelings that the music should be expanded and added to in the same way as contemporary music because people actually miss that; people find ... unaccompanied music too intense in a modern context; people are used to hearing a rhythm section, used to hearing a bass.*

With Planxty he remembers a particular moment when he made a decision about his own musical direction. It was during a recording when he was accompanying Liam O'Flynn:

> *I ended up after several hours playing a drone on a bouzouki, and what I was coming round to was that the tune was at its purest and its best without accompaniment. I mentally painted myself into a corner ... and it took me the rest of the day to get out of that, but it was a matter of making a decision on what way I was going to go. ... I remember making the decision that I accompany music, and Irish music can be accompanied without affecting its character.*[2]

This decision had implications for Donal's subsequent career in Irish music and has marked his work as a musician, arranger, and composer ever since.

Planxty had an identifiable sound early on, which derived from Christy's unique vocal style and personality, and the arrangements of tunes and songs. The instrumentation was bouzouki, mandolin, guitar and pipes.

2 Donal Lunny. Interview,

BIABH

Their sources for songs were other singers, especially old traditional singers, and old song collections. The search for songs led them back to the places where the oral tradition was still alive and the tradition benefited from this interest. Many old songs were taken out and dusted down and passed on to another generation.

In their playing and arrangement, both vocal and instrumental, they set about breaking new ground: 'everybody cared so much about the music and about the songs; I think unconsciously we were all trying to do definitive versions'.[3]

One of their 'definitive versions' was to segue from a vocal number into a traditional dance tune. This was Christy's idea and very new at the time: 'there was a huge gap between people's consciousness of Irish traditional music and people's awareness of Irish singing. Irish folk songs were sung all over the country, but traditional music wasn't played all over the country – it was happening at little sessions in pubs.'

Despite the earnestness and seriousness which underlay Planxty, fun, enjoyment and abandonment were part of the experience. Planxty gigs were more akin to rock gigs than folk sessions in terms of audience participation and approval. In the seventies the country was in a good mood and prepared to consider music on its merits.

Another innovation of Planxty's was the introduction of the bazouki to Irish music. Adapted to accommodate western chords by the addition of a fourth set of strings, it now has become *de rigueur*. Donal preferred bouzouki to guitar for accompanying traditional music: 'it's a bit emptier and didn't tend to fill the music or to colour the music as strongly as the guitar.... It has become an individual element of Irish music, which is no bad thing.'

THE DUBLINERS

In 1963 or thereabouts, even the band is not quite sure, the Dubliners were formed. On first appearances they could have been mistaken for a ballad group, but they were much more than this. Unlike many groups of the day they boasted one, and later two accomplished traditional players, Barney McKenna and John Sheehan. A crucial element in their image was the long hairy beards many of them sported. Their singers Ronny Drew and Luke Kelly were unorthodox, both in their singing and appearance. Both of them had a raw hard quality to their voices which gave the group its characteristic sound.

We played when it was dangerous
Barney McKenna of the Dubliners

3 Ibid.

The archetypal ballad
band of the sixties – The
Dubliners -- with the late
Luke Kelly (far right)

This was a welcome departure from the wholesome vocalising
and sweet harmonies favoured by some ballad singers.

Luke Kelly, who sadly died in his forties, possessed an
enormous voice, and sang with passionate intensity. He was
also a committed human rights activist. His choice of material
reflected his political opinions and identification with working-
class issues; songs like 'McAlpines Fusiliers', and 'The Hot
Asphalt' which dealt with the experiences of Irish navvies in
England. John Sheehan described the Dubliners' approach as:

> *Uninhibited ... I mean Ronny sang with a most peculiar
> voice, he didn't apologise to anybody for the way he sang,
> this was the voice that he found himself speaking with,
> and that's the way he sung ... Luke was a unique singer
> ... he had a great way of tackling a song and great
> phrasing and pacing.*

There was balance struck by the Dubliners between traditional music which had a rural root, and the songs, which
tended more towards urban folk. Despite the folk and trad tag
there was something gritty and urban about the Dubliners.
They sang work songs, rebel songs, bawdy songs, street songs,
love songs, and contemporary ballads.

In Barney's opinion folk music could offer more to people in
the sixties than, say, rock 'n' roll or pop:

*At that time most of the rock music was all 'He and She'
... it was all the one theme, you know what I mean;
whereas the folk theme brought out a wider spectrum.
You had songs and tunes about every walk in life.*

In 1967 the Dubliners recorded a traditional song they had
learned from 'Sean Nós' singer, Joe Heaney. It was called
'Seven Drunken Nights' and went into the British charts. The
'lads' duly made an appearance on *Top of The Pops*.

Twenty years later they made another appearance on the
same programme, this time in the company of The Pogues with
whom they had recorded a single. This was a much-sung
oft-hackneyed Irish comic song 'The Irish Rover'. Again the
Dubliners found themselves in the British charts to their
surprise:

*The 'Irish Rover' was recorded in about three or four
hours; it was a case of 'Right what key is it in? We'll try
G' ... and just recorded it and that was it. There was no
messing around for weeks and weeks like some of these
pop groups, you know, on thousands of pounds.*

The Dubliners' continuing success springs from their musical
abilities, choice of material, performances, and engaging personalities, but also as John McKenna says from: 'our general
attitude to life ... it's the ease of pace; there's no mad panic
at any stage ... our popularity had something to do with the
way we presented the whole thing. We stood up and here we
were, take us or leave us.'

CELTIC FOLKWEAVE

Planxty and the Dubliners presented two different but comp-
lementary faces of Irish folk music. Planxty experimented with
song arrangements, instrumentation, and accompaniment.
They looked for new ways to present old material (even though
there were one or two contemporary folk songs included).
The Dubliners' traditional arrangements did not stray from
standard presentation, but their singing style was unique as
were their collective and individual personalities.

The renewed interest in traditional and folk music in the
seventies produced a plethora of new bands, traditional folk,
and contemporary folk. It was also the hey-day of folk festivals,
the most memorable being at Ballisodare in Co. Sligo, and

Lisdoonvarna in Co. Clare. These were open-air events which took place over a weekend in the summer. There was also an international folk-festival circuit mainly in northern Europe: Germany, Switzerland, Denmark, and France. They catered for the large numbers of continental Europeans interested in folk and traditional music. Many of them travelled to Ireland to attend concerts, festivals and sessions, or simply to be in the place where traditional music was 'happening'.

The European market for traditional music made professional players out of many Irish musicians, traditional and otherwise. Part of the attraction of the European circuit of festivals, concerts and clubs was the prospect of meeting up with other musicians. The after-gig sessions were often looked forward to more than the gig itself.

'SUPERGROUPS'

The seventies was also the decade of the Irish touring band, the so-called 'supergroups'. One of the few who are still together, and with the same line-up, is Clannad.

They come from the Irish-speaking area of Donegal in the north-west of the country. Máire, Pól, and Ciarán grew up in Gaoth Dobhair, their mother's birthplace, and formed the band with the Padraig and Noel O'Dúgáin, while they were still in school. Their father, Leo Brennan, had run a dance band in the fifties and sixties and had involved the children in it when they were young. They were familiar through their mother with traditional songs in Irish, and with popular music through their father and radio and records. Máire was also a classically trained musician, and played the modern Irish harp.

Clannad's music mixed Irish traditional songs, in Irish, with jazz, classical, and folk idioms. They used no traditional instruments except for bodhrán and harp; and included such foreigners as double bass, silver flute, and bongos.

They developed an unmistakable sound from this instrumentation, but also from their unique vocal arrangements of Donegal songs. They toured very successfully in Europe for several years, gradually developing into a folk rock band with jazz and classical overtones.

'Texture' was a key component of Clannad's sound. To achieve this they exploited technical developments in sound recording. The vocal effects were enhanced by using synthesisers and voice-over dubbing. This became the dominant element in their presentation, on record and in performance.

Those festivals were great because ... you ended up playing with the people that were on the stage. It wasn't just getting on stage and doing a gig and just getting paid and going off; everybody just hung around for the three days and played and talked together and talked about music and it was great fun.[4]

4 Máire Ní Bhraonáin of Clannad

The effect was moody, ethereal, and atmospheric. The strangeness was heightened by the fact that they sang in Donegal Irish, or Gaelic as they call it.

In 1982 they were commissioned to write a theme for a TV series *Harry's Game*. The single which was released as a result reached number five in the British charts; the first song in Irish ever to do so.

When Bono of U2 heard 'Harry's Game' one day on his car radio, it stopped him in his tracks. He admires the way Clannad marry the 'technology of the modern recording studio to the fragility and frailty of the human voice. And yet they're working with samplers and highly sophisticated keyboards and synthesisers, so I think that bodes well for the future of Irish music.'

In 1986 Bono and Clannad collaborated on the 'Once in a Lifetime' single. Bono's powerful voice worked well as a foil for Máire's delicate vocals. This collaboration and Clannad's subsequent work in writing for film has given them a broad-based audience. According to Máire:

> *There's been a huge change in our audience, and I suppose it goes right across the board with all the kinds of music we have touched on ... but it's great to see the young people that you'd never see, coming to a Clannad gig, now coming and really enjoying what we're doing, especially the Gaelic songs. Because they hear the wonderful melodies, and you actually hear English bands, new English bands using Irish melodies as well because they're gorgeous and they're very strong.*

The vocal successes of Clannad in the seventies were equalled on the instrumental level by a new group, The Bothy Band. Planxty had disbanded in 1975 releasing Christy Moore to pursue a solo career. Donal Lunny, meanwhile, joined The Bothy Band. Within a short time of its establishment this became the most popular traditional band in the country.

Where Planxty had concentrated mainly on songs, The Bothy Band became famous for its arrangements of instrumental music. There were six players, three of whom were 'pure' traditional players. There were uilleann pipes, fiddle, flute, guitar, bouzouki, and clavinet (an electric keyboard instrument).

Donal described the 'Bothies' as 'six people lashing away at the tunes'. Energy levels were high in this band: 'That was the one thing which it was famous for; it was very fast and furious playing ... there was more emphasis on traditional tunes and there were more possibilities for arranging the music because of the fact that there were six players.'

The Bothies' arrangements and choice of tunes, and their way of playing set the standard for much ensemble playing in later years. Donal Lunny's use of the bouzouki as a rhythm instrument attracted many imitators. He describes his style as 'a combination of harmonies and rhythm and a certain amount of counterpoint.'

The bouzouki features in another Irish 'supergroup' which came together in the seventies – the Galway-based band, De Danann. While De Danann has had several first-rate singers over the years, it is famous for its driving, energetic style and melodic arrangements of dance tunes.

The two core members are fiddle player Frankie Gavin and bouzouki player and guitarist Alec Finn. Together they developed a recognisable 'De Danann sound'.

This is fast melodic fiddle playing set off by distinctive counter harmonies on the bouzouki, and accompanied by cello, bodhrán, flute, and button accordion.

Traditional dance music has always been important in De Danann's repertoire. They have also taken excursions into other styles and idioms. They once recorded an instrumental version of the Beatles' song 'Hey Jude' which they gave a fast and furious traditional interpretation. They followed this over

Alec Finn of De Danann, with daughter Heather

Frankie Gavin – member
of De Danann

the years with traditional interpretations of classical tunes, another Beatles' song, Jewish Klezmer music, and most recently black gospel music.

In New York, *Bringing It All Back Home* recorded them playing a traditional set, a set with the Donna Brown Singers from Harlem, and a set with Jewish Klezmer musician, Andy Statman. Andy Statman describes Klezmer music as 'the instrumental music of the Jews of Eastern Europe'.

Andy heard about De Danann through his involvement with an Irish recording company in New York. In their music he detected similarities to Klezmer. 'There is an obvious relationship superficially . . . in the phrasing and in the ornamentation . . . both are very highly ornamented forms, and some of the ornaments are the same.'

Out of this relationship came some new tunes for De Danann, 'The Jewish Reels', 'The Flatbush Waltz' and 'The Shepherd's Dream'. The tone and attack of the best Klezmer is well matched to De Danann.

Fundamentally De Danann remain committed to the roots of their music, and in particular to the memory of the great players like Coleman, Morrison, Killoran, and McKenna. For Frankie this connection is very important because: 'those were the people who knew how to play the music as far as I'm concerned; those are the only recordings that we have where we can get an idea of what the music really sounded like in those days, and they were certainly producing the goods'.

Over the years De Danann's singers included Mary Black, Dolores Keane, and Maura O'Connell, all of whom have gone on to have successful solo careers. Their current singer Elanor Shanley carries on the tradition of fine singing of traditional and popular ballads.

The other 'supergroup' which preceded De Danann, Planxty, and The Bothy Band, is the traditional group, The Chieftains. The leader of The Chieftains, piper Paddy Moloney was an original member of Seán Ó Riada's Ceoltóirí Chualann.

The Chieftains, of all the groups, retain the most traditional profile. There are two fiddle players, a flute player, a harper, a bodhrán player, and Paddy Moloney whom Ó Riada called 'one of the most gifted pipers in Ireland'. They are almost exclusively an instrumental band. They have performed Paddy Moloney's scores for film and theatre, and their most memorable work was with Van Morrison on the *Irish Heartbeat* album.

NEW DIRECTIONS

The 'supergroup' phenomenon of the seventies has passed. The Chieftains, The Dubliners, and De Danann are doyens of the folk and traditional scene, both as bands and as individual performers. The scene itself has changed and diverged as groups have broken up, re-formed, explored new territory, and individuals have gone on to have solo careers.

After some years singing traditional and folk material, Mary Black now has a flourishing career as a singer of more contemporary material, and has moved to a rock-influenced sound. Her singing style retains its traditional inflection and her choice of material tends to the ballad idiom.

For *Bringing It All Back Home* she recorded a song appropriately entitled 'No Frontiers' from her album of the same name. It has a thoroughly modern sound but a sensibility brought out by Mary's strong, pure voice, which is older.

Dolores Keane, also a former singer with De Danann, has made this transition too. Dolores comes from a family of traditional singers in Co. Galway. For *Bringing It All Back Home* she wore two hats, that of the traditional singer with her aunts Sarah and Rita; and that of the contemporary, singing Mick Hanley's song about Irish emigration in the nineties, 'My Love is in America'.

Mary and Dolores recorded two songs in Nashville with country singer Emmylou Harris for *Bringing It All Back Home*, 'The Grey Funnel Line' and 'Sonny'. These recordings are proof, if it is needed, that contemporary, traditional, and country music are still sympathetic to each other, and independent of each other at the same time.

Irish singers Dolores
Keane (centre) and Mary
Black (right) meet and
sing with Emmylou
Harris in Nashville,
Tennessee

PAUL BRADY

One Irish musician, whose career has woven in and out of traditional, folk, and rock 'n' roll, is Paul Brady. Like Donal Lunny, Paul's first musical influences were rock 'n' roll. While a student in Dublin in the mid-sixties, he played in several young rhythm and blues and rock 'n' roll bands. He met Donal Lunny and Mick Moloney around this time and through them came into contact with folk and traditional music. In 1967 he joined Mick in The Johnstons and made a thirteen-year commitment to traditional and folk music. (For much of this time he was based in England, and you can read more about this period of his life in Chapter 11).

The Johnstons' repertoire was traditional ballads, and contemporary folk songs. They had a successful career until their demise in 1974. Paul places The Johnstons right at the head of the folk revival in Ireland: 'I think that The Johnstons were really the first group ... to bring Irish singing to the population of Ireland since the Clancy Brothers.'

In 1974 Paul returned to Ireland to join Planxty. At this stage he says he went 'digging for lots of songs ... I was still primarily interested in being a traditional performer, a traditional singer, finding folk songs'. After Planxty broke up in 1975, Paul and Andy Irvine (also from Planxty) joined forces and produced an album of folk songs in 1976.

The *Andy Irvine/Paul Brady* album contained traditional songs collected by Paul and Andy and arranged for a variety of 'new' folk instruments; bouzouki, mandolin, cittern, etc. The superb vocal arrangements and harmonies achieved by the pair made this album a classic, which still sells.

Andy Irvine (top) and
Paul Brady – performing
traditional material in
the seventies

Both of them collected songs at source, that is, from traditional singers who sang in the traditional style, solo and
unaccompanied. Paul in particular collected many songs from
singers of his part of the country around County Tyrone in
Northern Ireland, where there is a very strong singing tradition.

In 1978 Paul made his last traditional album *Welcome Here
Kind Stranger*. With this album which included one of his most
popular songs, 'The Lakes of Ponchartrain', he felt he had gone
as far as he could go with traditional and folk idioms, both in
terms of arrangements and technically.

He felt that there was a side of his creative imagination that
was not being expressed in folk and traditional music. 'I was
finding parts of myself that were just new, so I found in me a
need to express this and to write songs. . . . I also wanted to get
back into playing rock music'.

In the space of a year he made a complete about-turn. In
1981 he brought out a rock album featuring his own songs and
an electric band. In the intervening nine years he has continued
to work in this idiom. He does not feel that he has left traditional music behind entirely: 'I think that the whole, experience of Irish music and the falling in love with songs made me
want to become a song writer, and when I saw people in
America, like Bob Dylan, were also coming out of that tradition
. . . that made me feel that I could start to do that too.'

Although he can isolate several musical strains in his own
work, one is pre-eminent: 'What comes out . . . is that Irish voice
with Irish inflections, with Irish accent, with Irish melodies. I
think it will always be the main thing in what I am.'

There are many other Irish artists and bands who have been
touched by contemporary music of all kinds, and who work in
non-traditional genres but 'speak with an Irish voice.' Luka
Bloom left Ireland in the eighties to restart a flagging career
as a singer-song writer, and met with success in America. In
the New York sessions for *Bringing It All Back Home* he sang
two songs, both of which bear upon Ireland in different ways.
'You couldn't have come at a Better Time' takes its opening
melody line from an Irish dance tune, 'The Kesh Jig', which
was popularised by The Bothy Band in the seventies. Luka is
accompanied on the recording by New York traditional fiddler
Eileen Ivers, playing an electric instrument, and by Colm
Murphy of De Danann on bodhrán.

'This is for Life' has no discernible Irish musical base, but it
has a strong Irish connection. It is the story of two lovers,
one Irish, one American, who 'transcend the system which

separates them'. Both songs are contemporary because: 'I don't come from a romantic Ireland, I come from a totally contemporary . . . modern Ireland with all its problems, and that's the Ireland I sing about, if I sing about Ireland at all.'

The Irish accent then can be in the musical or substantive construction, or both. In the case of Irishman Pierce Turner, it's in the melody and the singing style. Pierce now lives in New York. From musical beginnings which included a stint in a show band, he progressed to the avant-garde milieu inhabited by musicians like Philip Glass. He is a singer-song writer and recorded a song he calls 'All Messed Up' for *Bringing It All Back Home*. The melody which he plays on piano is constructed around a traditional Irish song 'Seán Ó Duibhir an Ghleanna' and the singing style is incantatory. Not surprising, because Pierce cites Seán Ó Riada (who recorded this on his last album) and plainchant as two major influences on his development as a musician.

'Cooler at the Edge' recorded by Scullion for *Bringing It All Back Home* is a song about emigration, a theme once again current in Irish song writing. Sonny Condell, song writer and founder of Scullion, writes and sings in modern idioms.

Musically Scullion has always defied categorisation. There was undoubtedly a strong folk influence, and the band covered traditional songs in the early days. Scullion was one of the first of the new-wave bands of the seventies to couple instruments like saxophone and uilleann pipes.

Luka Bloom records for *Bringing It All Back Home* in Hoboken, New Jersey

CROSSOVER

Paul Brady's break with the tradition was radical. Donal Lunny also wanted to break out of the traditional mainstream, but did not want to leave it behind. The Bothy Band had broken up in 1979, leaving him free to explore other dimensions of Irish music.

It was to the possibilities of merging rock and traditional idioms in music instrumentation that he turned his attention:

> *My interest at this time was applying [a rock rhythm section] to Irish music, maintaining an Irishness, if you like, to the style of music we were playing. It was extremely difficult for me to do this. However we did eventually figure out a way to play traditional tunes which I think held on to most of their personality and character.*

The subject of this experiment was Moving Hearts, set up in 1981 by Christy Moore and Donal Lunny. Christy Moore wanted a vehicle through which he could present contemporary songs, and Donal felt that this was compatible with his rock aspirations for traditional music.

Aside from Christy on vocals, Moving Hearts leaned heavily towards the instrumental. There was a saxophone player, a piper, bass and lead guitarists, drums and percussion, and Donal on a range of instruments, electric and acoustic bouzouki, and synthesisers. From its earliest days its attempt to make this connection between traditional music and electric rock was greeted with excitement and approval. Moving Hearts won a huge following amongst young people around the country. A Moving Hearts' gig was a heady mix of old music with a beat that had the audience on its feet for most of the gig.

They played in a driving, attacking style. Jazz, traditional and rock music all combined to provide an identifiable modern sound that was thoroughly Irish.

Unfortunately Moving Hearts was too big to be economically viable and it was forced to disband in 1984. The last album *The Storm* recorded posthumously, so to speak, in 1985, is exclusively instrumental. According to Donal Lunny it revealed 'a quality which hadn't been as apparent before. . . . I think the band actually came into its own for the first time with the instrumental music that we played.'

Donal continues to be preoccupied with these questions, and resolves them in new compositions and arrangements. He is

Moving Hearts in concert – jazz and rock meet traditional. Davy Spillane is the piper (right) and Donal Lunny on keyboards (far right)

Christy Moore (left)
records 'Fairytale of New
York' with Donal Lunny
for *Bringing It All Back
Home*

now convinced that Irish music is: 'closer to African or oriental
music than it is to American music ... the punctuation of
contemporary rhythms doesn't always suit Irish music.'

This line of thought is evidenced in a piece of music written
and performed specially for *Bringing It All Back Home*. 'April
3rd' is an instrumental piece whose melodic structure is based
on Irish traditional music. Rhythm is a major preoccupation.
The instrumentation is a combination of electric and acoustic,
including pipes, fiddle, keyboards, electric guitars, lead guitar
played by The Edge (of U2), bouzouki, bodhrán, and timpani
and percussion. The inclusion of several hand drums (bodhrán,
Egyptian hand drum, and percussion section) reflects this.
'April 3rd' is a tapestry of percussive 'running rhythms' and
melody. The exploration continues.

Donal is optimistic about traditional and contemporary Irish
music:

> *Musicians who have learned traditional music or been
> involved with traditional music play it the way it should
> be played; they'll have an Irish accent that will come
> through any context.... Traditional music has a place in
> contemporary music for that reason, because it can still
> be itself, still be alive and not affect the ongoing tradition
> of source music.*

CHAPTER ELEVEN

ACROSS THE WATER: THE IRISH IN BRITAIN

I was just about nineteen when I

landed on their shore

With my eyes big as headlights,

Like the thousands and thousands

who came before,

I was going to be something.[1]

PAUL BRADY

There is a substantial Irish community in Britain, one whose collective identification is with Ireland. Within this community Irish social customs, and culture, particularly Irish traditional music, persists. It was here in the Irish communities of the main British cities that the playing and teaching of traditional music was kept alive. Out of this community came a body of song which documented the lives of the working Irish.

The folk revival of the sixties focused attention on the music of this community, and for the first time Irish traditional music made an impact outside the Irish enclave. Later still in the eighties, second-generation Irish in Britain discovered in the Irish identity of their parents a rich cultural resource.

1 Paul Brady, 'Nothing but
the Same Old Story'

EARLY DAYS

By the eighteenth century small but distinct Irish enclaves had established themselves in many British cities. The famine years of 1845 to 1851 saw a huge increase in emigration to Britain and by 1861 there were 806 000 Irish in the country.

The cities of Scotland and the north of England were centres of densest concentration. At this time between eighteen and twenty-two per cent of the populations of Glasgow, Liverpool, and Dundee were Irish; in Salford and Manchester it was thirteen per cent.

These Irish did not assimilate easily. Many of the problems that assailed famine emigrants to America confronted Irish immigrants in Britain. They were impoverished, unskilled and often in bad health. Their customs, language, and practice of congregating together in slums alienated them from British society.

What work they found was likely to be unskilled or semi-skilled work in construction, on the railways, or on the dock-side. Factory work in the sugar and textile industry absorbed many, and the women worked in domestic service and laundries. Over the years the Irish entrenched themselves in these occupations, and operated closed shop systems like their counterparts in America. This and the fact that they tended to reproduce Irish systems of social organisation consolidated the conservative nature of the Irish community. In addition, the Irish were Catholic and bore no loyalty to the country which they had settled in. Britain in their eyes was the instigator of emigration.

Built into the Irish immigrant experience in Britain, these factors worked against integration.

Once the Irish established themselves more firmly in their communities, Irish societies and clubs sprang up. They tended to be organised along nativist lines and were a focus for collective Irish identification. Nationalist preoccupations in Ireland were mirrored in Britain as was the revival of interest in Irish culture. At the turn of the century, organisations like the Gaelic League were associated with the Irish cultural revival. League-organised social activities like dances and musical evenings kept the connection with Ireland alive.

The Gaelic League in London is credited with the introduction of céilí dancing in 1897 at an event in the Bloomsbury Hall. (This form of group dancing has been described in greater detail in Chapter 5). The members of organisations like the Gaelic League were for the most part educated and literate. They regarded events like céilís as outlets for cultural expression otherwise unavailable to them.

First, according to Barry Taylor, to use the title 'céilí band' was the Tara Céilí Band which was first established as a dance band to play at St Patrick's Day celebrations in the Sarsfield Club in Notting Hill in 1918. The club was established in 1890 and some Irish dances had been taught there by a dancing master, Padraig O'Keane. The céilí band was put together by a second-generation London-Irishman Frank Lee. He recruited twenty musicians in all and called the resultant band the Tara Céilí Band. Two thousand people attended that night, establishing the popularity of this kind of event for a further thirty years.

As an indication of how close the association was between cultural and political identification with Ireland, Frank Lee's involvement with the I R A forced him to leave England a year later. He went to New York where he teamed up with the legendary Sligo fiddler, Michael Coleman. In time he returned to London where he once again took the baton as leader of the Tara Céilí Band.

By the thirties, commercial interests were involved in the organisation of céilí type dances for the Irish in Britain. There was a string of Irish clubs in the main Irish centres in London, perhaps the most famous being the Garryowen in Shepherds Bush Road. Queues formed outside the Garryowen long before the eight o'clock opening and those not admitted by ten past eight were turned away.

The Garryowen Band and all the other bands who played for these dances were made up of recently-arrived Irish traditional players, second-generation players who read music, and session men. As for the repertoire: 'the natural conservatism of the exile [and] the natural desire to be reminded of the homeland, ensured that the music purveyed in these establishments was a hybrid affair – a mixture of traditional Irish and mid-twenties ... popular dance music.'[2]

Paddy Taylor, a traditional musician who played in the Garryowen, described some of the other London musicians as emanating from the fife and drum bands of the teens and twenties. 'Each district like Wapping, round that area, they all had had their own bands – they used to have competitions and everything – and very Irish you know, my God, although they probably never saw the sky over Ireland.'[3]

2 Barry Taylor, 'The Irish Ceilidh – A Break with Tradition?' *Dal gCais*, 1984.

3 Alan Ward, 'Paddy Taylor – An Individual Musician', *Traditional Music*, No. 2, late 1975

There was not much outlet then for the playing of 'straight' traditional music. This came later, after the Second World War when Comhaltas Ceoltóirí Eireann established branches in Britain and promoted traditional music at organised sessions, as well as classes and Fleadheanna Cheoil.

Paddy Taylor, who became involved in Comhaltas activities early on, recalled that it was difficult in the beginning to get sessions going in London. There were problems finding suitable venues and attracting a crowd. From the start the organisation was keen to emphasise the community aspect of Irish music. 'We didn't give a damn,' said Paddy, 'whether they were good, bad or indifferent. Everybody was welcome ... so long as they [had] the inclination to play. And you always hear something in somebody's playing if you listen.'

From these beginnings grew a lively traditional music scene in London and other cities with Irish communities. When emigration peaked again in the fifties London became an increasingly popular location for Irish immigrants. Sociologist Liam Ryan cites an additional motivation for emigration in 'the pull of those already away'. The depressed state of rural Ireland compared unfavourably with news of large pay packets and the 'crack' to be found in the Irish communities in England. (He offers a definition of 'crack' as the 'jovial company of one's own people'.)

By the time Sligo flute player Roger Sherlock arrived in London in 1952 he was able to establish a band which played five nights a week. This was in the Galtymore ballroom and pub complex in Kilburn. 'It still wasn't enough to make a living out of,' he says, 'nothing like it'. He worked by day, 'six days a week [with] the pick and shovel ... mostly roads you know which was hard work'. The massive reconstruction pro-grammes undertaken in post-war Britain absorbed thousands of Irish workers. Unskilled labour was what was needed and the majority of Irish male emigrants fell into this category.

Factory work was also available, and for women there was domestic and hotel work. Many women also availed themselves of training opportunities in nursing and in doing so progressed one scale up the social ladder.

For Roger Sherlock and other musicians 'life was pretty hectic, because you had to be up at six in the morning, and then from the late sessions ... sometimes we didn't get back until two or three o'clock, so you didn't have much sleep.' As well as organised dances like those in the Galtymore, there were also sessions of traditional music based around pubs.

Oh mother dear, I'm over here, I'm never coming back, What keeps me here is the pint of beer, the women and the crack.

Roger Sherlock met the piper Willie Clancy from Clare at a pub session in the Black Cap in Camden Town. Musicians congregated there on Sunday mornings and evenings, and this is where they played for themselves. The late Willie Clancy, one of the master pipers of the twentieth century, had also emigrated to London in the fifties. He was later to return to live in his native town of Miltown Malby in Co. Clare where he died in 1973.

Miltown Malby is now the location of a major event in the Irish traditional music calendar, the Willie Clancy Summer School, popularly known as 'The Willie Week'. Thousands, coming from all parts of the world, attend the sessions and classes run by the school.

Willie Clancy was only one of a number of important Irish musicians to be found in Britain, especially London, in the fifties and sixties. According to Alan Ward who has made a study of traditional music in London: 'at one time or another most of the great figures in contemporary Irish music could be heard playing regularly in Camden Town or Fulham'.[4]

The great Connemara 'Sean Nós' singer Joe Heaney lived in London before emigrating to America, and the Clare fiddler Bobby Casey still lives in London and plays regularly with Roger Sherlock. Traditional music is now flourishing in England. Comhaltas has established branches in most cities,

Bobby Casey, traditional musician from Co. Clare, who now lives and works in London

4 Ibid.

and children are taught by older players in classes run by this and other organisations. Many of the children are prepared for the annual Fleadheanna run by Comhaltas.

The high point in the competition year is the All Ireland Fleadh Cheoil. Like their American counterparts, teachers regard working towards competitions as good motivation. Eilish Byrne, who teaches traditional fiddle at the Irish Centre in Camden Town, is a second-generation player who has won the All Britain and All Ireland competition in the past. These days she devotes most of her time to teaching.

Pupils in the Irish Centre are taught the rudiments of staff notation but are then 'weaned off it' and learn their tunes orally from their teachers. According to Siobhan O'Donnell, a young flute teacher at the Centre, the children are developing their own style by the age of eleven. 'They'll come out,' says Siobhan, 'with their own ideas of tunes that we've given them, maybe not so much copying what I'm doing but more experimenting themselves ... basically doing the ornamentation and the more technical side of it, thinking about the tunes themselves.'

This new generation of traditional players in England ensures that the playing tradition will stay alive and be renewed as long as there is an Irish community to support it.

The activities of Comhaltas Ceoltóirí Eireann give impetus and encouragement to the playing of traditional music in Britain. The flourishing pub sessions, classes, and concerts which were part of the traditional music scene were given added life in the sixties and seventies by the folk-music revival. The upsurge of interest in the traditional music of Britain, American folk and blues, also threw a light on Irish music. Musicians from outside the tradition would draw on an Irish traditional music source, thereby bringing it to a wider British audience.

A young pupil at the Irish Centre in Camden Town, London

BRITISH FOLK

A leading figure of the revival in Britain was 'Ewan MacColl', real name, James Miller. Of Scottish parentage, MacColl had grown up in the industrial town of Salford. He was politicised early on in life by his father who was a radical free-thinker, and was involved in the workers' movement. His mother was a singer who knew hundreds of traditional songs, and from her MacColl developed the style of the traditional

A leading figure of the
British folk revival –
Ewan MacColl

ballad singer. MacColl went on to become involved in running
folk clubs in London. These clubs, like the Scots Hoose and
the Singers Club, were based around London's bohemian Soho
district. MacColl was a singer and song writer of considerable
talent as well as a playwright and polemicist.

He believed that folk song was a powerful medium, a social
catalyst and expression of working-class solidarity. He also
passionately believed that popular song should reflect social
reality and become 'real folk' songs. His own songs exemplified
this. They take their form from the ballad tradition and their
subjects from the lives of ordinary people, working people, and
travelling people.

His pioneering work in radio in traditional music brought
him into contact with traditional singers and musicians all over
Britain and Ireland. He was involved in another series of
programmes called *Radio Ballads*. These were programmes
recorded 'in the field' which incorporated recordings of traditional music and new songs composed by MacColl himself.
These radio ballads were thematic in structure, and dealt with
topics like seafaring, travelling people, and so on. Out of this
work came some of MacColl's best songs, 'The Travelling
People', 'The Shoals of Herring', 'Dirty Old Town' and the
'Tunnel Tigers'. All of these songs entered the tradition and
became folk standards. They dealt with life on the road for
travelling people, the hard life of trawlermen in the 'Shoals of
Herring'. This song was a popular number in the Clancy

Brothers' repertoire. MacColl was reported to be delighted when he heard this song referred to as 'The Shores of Erin' by an Irishman. He felt then that it had achieved true folk anonymity in this process.

MacColl was enormously important as a source of songs for young folk singers. The late Luke Kelly of The Dubliners spent his early singing career in England learning from MacColl, as did singer Christy Moore. His songs remain in the folk repertoire. Many of them have achieved the status of folk classics, like 'Dirty Old Town' recorded by The Pogues and the uncharacteristic love song, 'The First Time Ever I Saw Your Face' which was a hit for Roberta Flack.

In MacColl's wake came a host of singers and groups interested in both the pure tradition and in contemporary folk. For the first time Irish traditional musicians began to be considered by folk enthusiasts who now frequented pubs like The White Hart in Fulham where 'pure' traditional music was played.

The other big early folk movement was skiffle, its principal exponent being Lonnie Donegan who had a huge hit with a Leadbelly song 'The Rock Island Line' in 1956. Over one million copies were sold. It was the first British single to make the US Top Ten. The result was a skiffle craze in England which even claimed John Lennon and Paul McCartney. Their first band, The Quarrymen, was a skiffle band. Donegan went on to record and popularise Woody Guthrie's repertoire in Britain and in this way introduced American traditional and contemporary folk music to a British (and Irish) audience.

Singer-songwriter Richard Thompson remembers the atmosphere of this time as being one of possibilities:

> *We played everything. There was a lot of work around so we tried to cover all possible bases, so if someone wanted a blues band we could be a blues band, if they wanted a jug band we could be a jug band, we could be a folk group, we could do anything really. It was exciting, good training.*[5]

Folk and traditional music combined in Thompson's later work with the band, Fairport Convention. Fairport was regarded as a ground-breaking band in the sixties and early seventies. Its daring mixture of rock and folk idioms, innovative arrangements and instrumentation, the combination of traditional and contemporary material went far beyond anything heard before.

5 Richard Thompson, Interview, *BIABH*

Eventually Richard became more rock-orientated, although his songs remain rooted in the ballad tradition.

The two Thompson songs recorded in Nashville for *Bringing It All Back Home* are contemporary ballads of striking melodic beauty. Irish singer Mary Black, formerly known as a folk artist, joined Richard on both, while traditional singer Dolores Keane sings on the first.

The 'Dimming of the Day', a love song, has a vocal construction more akin to traditional song than contemporary rock. Its lovely decorated melody line, folk-song cadences and acoustic backing make categorising it as either a 'rock' or 'folk' song impossible. This is no bad thing. Rigid classifications like folk and rock do not accurately represent Richard Thompson's material.

> *This old house is falling down around my ears*
> *I'm drowning in the river of my tears*
> *When all my will is done you hold me sway*
> *I need you at the dimming of the day.*

The second song, 'Waltzings for Dreamers', falls more easily into the category of country ballad, and is in 3/4 waltz time. The appeal of these songs is instant and enduring. Richard Thompson represents all that is best in the British music tradition. He has absorbed elements of folk, traditional and rock music and given the contemporary music tradition something unique and beautiful.

Richard Thompson and Mary Black recording for *Bringing It All Back Home* in Nashville

THE SAME OLD STORY

Paul Brady was about twenty-two when he arrived in London, as a professional musician with The Johnstons folk group. With Irish chart success behind them, The Johnstons decided to base themselves in England to take advantage of the burgeoning folk-music revival there. They had three very successful years in Britain, gigging, recording, and making television appearances. Their repertoire was a mixture of contemporary folk and traditional songs with an emphasis on strong instrumental arrangements. Like many other trad and folk artists of the time they were influenced by Ewan MacColl and recorded and had a hit with his song 'The Travelling People'. When not travelling or gigging Paul lived 'in an Irish ghetto area of Kilburn ... I used to associate with Irish people all the time (I didn't know any English people) who went to Irish bars and played Irish music'. In doing this he was conforming to the stereotype of the newly-arrived Irishman in England. Typical, too, of the Irish who arrived in England for the first time was the tendency to come without money, job, or accommodation secured. Liam Ryan has described the situation of the Irish immigrant as a problem 'compounded with sheer irresponsibility. The man who wouldn't dream of going to Dublin without a job and place to stay often stepped readily off the train at Paddington or Euston with no skills, no job, no money and nowhere to live.'[6]

Paul was not in this kind of desperate situation, but he was struck by the numbers of Irishmen who had come over years before:

> *They'd go to England to make their pile and come back home and buy the cottage in the west of Ireland.... But they never managed to extricate themselves ... they end up in the middle of London somewhere in pubs drinking themselves to death because they know now that they're never really going to get back ... you knew they were never ever going to go back to Ireland ... and that made me very sad.*

Many years later when Paul had returned to rock music and was writing his own material, he wrote a song based on those experiences. He called it 'Nothing but the Same Old Story'. In it he tried to describe the feelings of a lost Irish soul in England.

This soul is angry, beaten and defeated. His dreams have disappeared; he will live the rest of his life as an outcast. The only relief he finds is in drinking:

Hey Johnny can't wait until Saturday night,
Got a thirst that's raging,
Know a place where we can put that right
Wash away the confusion,
Hose down this fire inside. But look out!
'Cause I'll tear you into pieces if you cross me.

Many Irish immigrants in London today stare the reality of this song in the face. Nor is Paul Brady the only song writer to document the loneliness and despair of the forgotten Irish. The statistics still show a disproportionately high propensity of Irish people in Britain to be admitted to mental hospitals, to be involved in crime, to be homeless and dependent on social welfare. This is the milieu in which Shane MacGowan of The Pogues finds inspiration for songs.

THE POGUES AND SHANE MacGOWAN

Journalist Eamonn McCann writing in *Hot Press* in 1988 defined The Pogues as 'Irish music viewed through the prism of a North London sensibility'. The Pogues and Shane MacGowan took traditional and folk-based Irish music and fired it in the crucible of modern Irish emigration. They emerged in the early eighties as a band who played a chaotic set of stock Irish rebel tunes in London clubs. From the beginning they were iconoclasts. Their name The Pogues is an abbreviation of their original name The Pogue Mahones. Pogue Mahone, or 'pog mo thoin' is a put-down in Irish, literally 'kiss my arse'. The name-change came about when a Gaelic-speaking television producer rumbled it. Elvis Costello remembers hearing them in the early days: 'I first saw The Pogues in a ... sort of arts club.... They did half a dozen songs all in G at the same speed, total gala stuff; it was hard to pick up what was going on among it.'

What had happened was that Irish ballads, like those popularised by the Clancys, had met punk. Pogues' music represented children of the sixties 'born after Carlow building workers had set up homes with Mayo nurses'. They were assimilated to the extent that they had been reared, educated and socialised in Britain. They rejected the anodyne ballad culture of the Irish communities their parents identified with. The Pogues showed a way in which they could be Irish in Britain. The music was exciting and contemporary in form and content, yet it was culturally familiar also. Elvis Costello describes The Pogues' music as 'a promise of a good time'. Off-stage and on, The Pogues disported themselves like archetypal Paddies, with a reputation for hard drinking, bad manners, and disdain for personal appearance. The Pogues' music, attitudes and lifestyle outraged a wide range of people from parents to traditionalists.

For Elvis Costello The Pogues were the antidote to the stultification imposed on folk music by purists. He respects traditional musicians who 'have no truck with commercialism and don't desire greater attention [but] follow their chosen line in their own way'. But: 'then you get other people who sort of resented The Pogues ... because they've been trying to grab a bigger audience and they've been never able to succeed; ... they can't see that it's basically dead end what they're doing'. For these reasons he engaged The Pogues as support band for his tour. Later he worked with them as producer and in 1987 produced 'The Wild Rover' single.

Elvis did not so much produce 'The Wild Rover' as 'deconstruct' it:

> *I got what I thought was one degree of revenge in the recording ... of The Pogues doing 'The Wild Rover'. Something I'd wanted to do for a long time was beat that song up. Although it has fond memories for some people ... it was the bane of my life when I was first starting out 'cos some half wit could get up and sing that song at the end of the night and go down a storm ... There'd be a few of us there with songs, however good they were, but at least we'd have written them ourselves.*

The Pogues these days depend heavily on Shane MacGowan for songs, and his early promise as a song writer has been realised. For Christy Moore who recorded MacGowan's 'Fairytale of New York' for *Bringing It All Back Home* 'he's the one writer of all the modern writers that I can connect with ... he just has ways of describing things that I can really relate to; he can sum up something in a way that I can understand.' 'The Pogues', remarked Elvis Costello, 'saved folk from the folkies.'

It was Christmas Eve babe, in the drunk tank, An old man said son I won't see another one.[6]

6 Shane MacGowan, 'Fairytale of New York'

Contemporary folksong
writer Shane MacGowan
of The Pogues

MISCHIEVOUS GHOST: ELVIS COSTELLO

Elvis Costello, real name Declan MacManus, does not identify
himself as Irish, although he was born into the Irish community
of Birkenhead on Merseyside. The MacManuses had emigrated
from 'God knows where' in Ireland three generations ago and
settled there. His grandfather trained as a musician in the
British army. His father, Ross MacManus, was a professional
singer with the Joe Loss Orchestra, a popular English dance
band. Elvis grew up in London where his earliest musical
influences were rock 'n' roll.

It was a musical household; his father who had started out
as a jazz trumpet player had wide musical tastes, and as a

dance-band singer had to do a lot of covers. Irish folk music was also played and sung around the house, but he came to dislike the English folk scene because of its puritanical stance. Nevertheless his first gigs as a singer-song writer were in folk clubs. He recalls on one occasion that Ewan MacColl was in the first row of the audience but fell asleep during his set. In the post-punk era after the Sex Pistols had turned popular music upside down, Elvis formed one of the most important new-wave bands of the day, The Attractions. His output of songs and albums since that time has been prolific: between 1977 and 1990, eleven LPs plus two compilations.

Elvis Costello – rock, traditional and classical preoccupations

His work reflects his wide range of preoccupations and musical interests from jazz to country to traditional. His most recent album *Spike the Beloved Entertainer* featured over thirty-two musicians, including Roger McGuinn and Chrissie Hynde. Six Irish musicians worked on the album, most of them in the traditional idiom.

'Mischievous Ghost' is a song specially written by him for *Bringing It All Back Home*. It does not consciously set out to be an 'Irish' song: 'I wanted to do something different . . . I didn't think I had the authority to take a traditional piece and sing it my own way, so I thought I'd write something that maybe made some sort of comment on one element of [the] story'.

The mischievous ghost of the title is the dead poet who in life outgrew his own legend and died before it could catch up with him. His audience are so scandalised by this ungenerous act that they dig him up, rehabilitate him and put him once again on public show. It is says Elvis 'a life after death song'.

Musically it is 'a collision between a discipline like chamber music and a melody derived somewhat from traditional music'. Vocals are by Elvis with a traditional-type refrain sung by Mary Coughlan. The string backing is overlain by uilleann pipes played by Davy Spillane. The result opens up an area bounded by rock, folk singing and classical music.

'Mischievous Ghost' is in line with Elvis Costello's personal philosophy of music:

> *I started with rock 'n' roll and you don't really think of it in a scholarly way, then you start to take it apart like a child with a toy and you see that there's blues and there's country. . . . Then you go back from country into American music, and you go back from American folk music and you end up in Scotland or Ireland eventually.*

CHAPTER TWELVE

THE LIGHT OF OTHER DAYS

I don't think it's possible to blend Irish traditional music and European art music. You can only interface them

MICHEÁL Ó SÚILLEABHÁIN

IRISH TRADITIONAL MUSIC AND CLASSICAL MUSIC

As we have seen, Ireland did not have a strong European art-music tradition. This kind of music was generally the preserve of a ruling English élite, and later of an urban middle class. Irish traditional music developed along separate lines. It was largely confined to the native Irish and its defining characteristics remained and remain unchanged; it is an orally transmitted form. European art music on the other hand depends on musical notation; it is a literate form. With one exception, in the eighteenth century, there was little connection between the two.

Musical literacy has been advancing in Ireland since the seventeenth century. In the past thirty years the process has accelerated, with the result that traditional and European art music have been brought face to face.

Traditional music and musicians are beginning to inhabit the western art-music arena. Traditional music has attracted the creative imaginations of musicians and composers like Seán Ó Riada in the sixties, and more recently Mícheál Ó Súilleabháin, Shaun Davey and John Cage, the avant-garde composer. Common ground is opening up between the two traditions; musical literacy or lack of it is no longer a barrier to expression.

One form of Irish traditional music which has elements of a classical or high-art form attaching to it, is 'Sean Nós' singing. For this reason I wish to consider it under the classical heading, although it has no connection with the European classical tradition, and is embedded in oral folk tradition.

SEAN NÓS SINGING

In Chapter 1 we saw how dependent 'Sean Nós' singing is on the Irish language, and how its fortunes as an art form were affected historically by the encroachment of English as the spoken language in Ireland. 'Sean Nós' is rooted in the Irish-speaking world and the repertoire is in that language with a few exceptions. It did not survive the colonising effect of English, nor its transplantation in America or Britain.

The origins of 'Sean Nós' singing are obscure but it seems probable that elements of it emerged out of the bardic poetry of the middle ages.

Bards and musicians had been members of the great households of the old aristocracy which went into terminal decline after the Battle of Kinsale in 1610. The poet was the principal figure in the musical retinue of such a household. He composed poems which were performed by the bard to the accompaniment of the harp. (The two roles eventually merged and the later poets were also harpers). The poems were chanted or sung rather than recited.

As there was no written music at this time, we have no idea what the poem or accompaniment sounded like. Once this old order collapsed, the poet/harpers were redundant. The new order was English speaking and increasingly musically literate. It made no room for an archaic form in an unknown language.

It seems likely that remnants of the vocal tradition were then subsumed into the folk singing of the time. Séan Ó Riada concluded, for example, that the practice of variation, central to 'Sean Nós' singing derives in part from bardic practices. Long songs of twenty verses and more had to be varied to avoid being monotonous. The variations of necessity had to be on a small scale or the structure would become top-heavy. The skill of the singer, then as now, lay in the ability to make these subtle changes. This in turn makes demands on the listener. The variations have to be recognised to be appreciated. Seán Ó Riada compared the 'true aficionado of Seán Nós' to the Spanish aficionado of bull-fighting: 'he applauds each well-made variation just as the Spaniard applauds each well-executed pass with a cape'.[1]

The importance of variation in instrumental tradition is mirrored in 'Sean Nós' singing. Much of the instrumental music, as we have seen, is dance music, so a steady rhythm or beat is necessary. This is not the case in 'Sean Nós'. It is not the sort of music to tap one's toes to. The 'Sean Nós' singer sings at his or her own pace. The variation chosen by the singer and the metre of the lyrics will dictate the pace at which the song moves.

Unlike the sung poems of the bardic order, 'Sean Nós' singing is unaccompanied. It relies totally for effect on the skill, technique and personality of the singer and is always a solo form. It demands of the singer 'an artistic understanding beyond the demands made on the average European singer. This is because a good deal of each song is improvised and the singer must know how to improvise in the proper style.'[2]

The Connemara Galetacht is renowned for its rich 'Sean Nós' tradition and is one of the few places left in Ireland where the 'Sean Nós' is still part of the living tradition. Josie Sheáin, Jack MacDhonnacha and Sara Grealish who recorded for *Bringing It All Back Home* were born in the Connemara Gaeltacht and are acclaimed 'Sean Nós' singers. Sarah's two sisters are also well known 'Sean Nós' singers as was Josie Sheáin Jack's father. Josie Sheáin Jack teaches 'Sean Nós' singing to local children in Carna. He reckons that some of the songs he passes on are more than two hundred years old: 'They're more or less the same as they were two hundred years ago.'

New songs are added to the tradition but he favours the older ones. The contemporary 'Sean Nós' songs are 'not as rich as the older ones; the language used in them and the music are probably not as good'.

There is evidence that the 'Sean Nós' influence has spread out into more contemporary musical forms. Liam Ó Maonlaí of The Hothouse Flowers has spoken of the debt he owes to 'Sean Nós' in developing his singing style. This sensibility which Tony MacMahon describes as 'intensely lyrical' is evident in Liam's approach to contemporary material. But he

1 Seán Ó Riada, *Our Musical Heritage*, p. 24

2 Ibid., p. 23

also sings 'straight' 'Sean Nós' and recorded a love song in this style for *Bringing It All Back Home* – 'Iníon an Fhaoit ón Ghleann'.

As I have mentioned in Chapter 9, another singer more usually associated with rock music than 'Sean Nós', Sinéad O'Connor recorded 'I am Stretched on your Grave', an unaccompanied song strongly influenced by this style. The original song in Irish, 'Ta mé sínte ar do thuama' was sung for *Bringing It All Back Home* by Diarmuid Ó Súilleabháin, who is from the west Cork Gaeltacht of Cúil Aodha. This area is renowned for its fine singers. Love songs such as these are the most numerous type of traditional song in Irish: 'When the Irish speaker sings ... he speaks of love, he speaks lyrically, he speaks of the now, and it's all linked to feeling and emotion ... and a very strong sense of place.'[3]

The future of 'Sean Nós' singing will depend ultimately on whether the Gaeltacht and the Irish language prosper. Right now it is at a critical stage in its history. Emigration has hit the Gaeltacht hard, and if the supply of young people falls below replacement level, the future of Irish as a spoken language will be jeopardised as will 'Sean Nós'. Other factors like modernisation, mass communications, and the spread of English are also making inroads on this unique and ancient tradition.

THE HARPING TRADITION

Because the ancient harp music of Ireland was not written down and because we know very little about the way in which the instrument was played, we have no clear idea of what the music sounded like. We know that the old Irish harps were metal-strung and played with the nails but we know little of the technique.

What little we do know about the harp music was made possible by the advent of musical literacy.

Turlough Carolan was an important figure in Irish harping. He is known as 'the last of the Irish harpers' although this is not so. Born in 1670 when the decline of the harping tradition was well under way, he did manage to make a living as a professional harper and enjoyed the patronage of wealthy households and in particular of a Mrs MacDermott Roe. Carolan is important because he stands at the crossroads where ancient tradition and new European art music met. He succeeded in straddling the old Gaelic world and the new English-speaking establishment.

[3] Mícheal Ó Súilleabháin. Interview, *BIABH*

Moving in Anglo-Irish circles Carolan came into contact with the popular art music of the day, namely the works of the Italian composers Vivaldi and Corelli whose pupil Geminiani lived in Dublin. Carolan's works reflect this Italianate influence and for this reason can be set apart from Irish harp music which preceded it. Coming from an oral tradition, and with the handicap of blindness, he mastered aspects of baroque composition.

Irish harp music was diatonic rather than chromatic. The instrument, which did not have a full chromatic scale, did not adapt easily to the chromatic music becoming increasingly popular throughout the seventeenth century.

For this reason Carolan's tunes played on modern instruments sound more baroque than traditional. On the Irish harp which Carolan played, his compositions would have retained a traditional feel: 'Though he did imitate the art music of the period in writing tunes, when it came to playing them, the nature of his instrument was such that the melodies sounded best when accompanied in the traditional harp way.'[4]

Carolan differed from the harpers who preceded him in having his compositions published in his own lifetime. The eighteenth century was 'the first century in which Irish music was published in any considerable quantity and it was the first century in which Irish music was published in Ireland'.[5]

Irish music published in the eighteenth century did not actually represent the repertoire of traditional music of the day. As Nicholas Carolan points out in his paper on music publishing, 'what are overwhelmingly represented in print are instrumental melodies and song airs of a type that the non-native ear found attractive'. We can be grateful that Carolan's music was included in this designation.

Máire Ní Chathasaigh is an Irish harper who plays what she calls a 'neo-Irish harp': it looks like the old Irish harp but it is constructed using modern methods ... the thing that makes it an Irish harp is that it has a curved front fore-pillar that is typical of Irish harps from the earliest times'.

For *Bringing It All Back Home* she recorded a Carolan tune, 'Carolan's Farewell to Music'. Legend has it that he composed it on his death bed:

> *It's interesting from a musical point of view in that it shows no baroque influence whatever ... it's very very Irish in its whole style and conception and emotion. It's interesting that it should be his last composition, that he went back to his roots so to speak at the end.*

4 Gráinne Yeats, 'The Rediscovery of Carolan' in *The Achievement of Seán Ó Riada*, ed. Bernard Harris and Grattan Freyer (Irish Humanities Centre and Keohanes, 1981)

5 Nicholas Carolan, 'The Most Celebrated Irish Tunes. The Publishing of Music in the Eighteenth Century', Ó Riada Memorial Lecture No. 5 (The Irish Traditional Music Society, UCC, 1990)

The next landmark in the history of harp music was the Belfast Harpers festival of 1792. The last remaining harpers – about a dozen in all – were assembled in Belfast for the purpose of having their music transcribed and preserved. The organisers of the festival were patriotic-minded men who also represented well the eighteenth-century interest in antiquities and folklore. They were concerned that this music would perish with the last of these harpers, who were old even then. It is reported also that only one played in the old way with long crooked fingernails.

Edward Bunting, then a young man, was engaged to transcribe the music. He was affected so deeply by this event that he dedicated the rest of his life to the collection and transcription of traditional Irish music.

He went on to publish three volumes of collections. The first published in 1796 was the fruits of the harping festival and other harp music he recorded 'in the field'. Unfortunately Bunting was trained in the modern art-music system of major and minor scales. His transcriptions of harp compositions sometimes put them in keys which would have been impossible on the Irish harp.

It is still a valuable record though. Without it we would have little record of this music or how it was played.

Bunting's collections, and the work of the collectors who followed him – Petrie and Joyce principally – were published and presented not to traditional musicians who did not read music, but to a middle- and upper-class audience who were far removed from it. This audience was interested in arrangements of Irish airs and melodies which could be adapted to the modern scale system. This arranged form of Irish music reached its high point of expression in the works of Tom Moore in the nineteenth century. Moore used the old airs in Bunting's collection as the basis for his own lyrics, which enjoyed tremendous popularity in the English-speaking world. Through this international acclaim and the universal popularity of songs like 'Believe Me if All those Endearing Young Charms' and 'Oft in the Stilly Night', 'Moore's Melodies', so called, came to be regarded as typically Irish.

SEÁN Ó RIADA AND HARP MUSIC

Ó Riada who had been trained in western art-music forms was interested in many aspects of Irish music and performance, one of which was old Irish harping and harp music. He scoured old collections and manuscripts and made innovative arrangements of harp music for performance with his ensemble Ceoltóirí Chualann. He disliked the tone of the modern Irish harp, and in the absence of an authentic instrument chose a harpsichord. The harpsichord is metal-strung like the old harps, and the strings are plucked by quills. It does not have the resonance of the old harp nor is it confined to a seven-note scale. In any event Ó Riada was not using the harpsichord to recreate the sound of the old harp. On the contrary:

> *He used the harpsichord largely as he would have used the piano, with full chords and plentiful use of modulations ... the two-tone colour of the instrument suits traditional music very well, but it is a new sound, a new traditional instrument in its own right.*[6]

The harpsichord was always a dominant element in the performances of Ceoltóirí Chualann. Ó Riada used it as a solo instrument, as continuo, and for accompaniment to singing.

Towards the end of his life he made a solo album of traditional music on harpsichord. Graínne Yeats, who is a harper, has identified a significant change in Ó Riada's approach in this album. He had come into possession, near the end of his life, of a nineteenth-century traditional harp. Experimenting on this had brought him nearer an understanding of the technique and style of old harping. This is evident on the album which is called *Ó Riada's Farewell* and is his last recording. Graínne Yeats feels that he would have advanced further in this direction had he lived to continue his explorations.

Very few people today use the harpsichord to the extent that Ó Riada did. Harp music though, particularly that of Carolan, has a dominant place in the repertoire of traditional and some non-traditional players. It is played on a variety of instruments from guitars, to flutes, fiddles, mandolins, and bouzouki. Carolan's name today is known by people who have but a nodding acquaintance with Irish music. It is surely remarkable that a music which was once accessible to none but a small ruling élite should now be so universally popular.

Mícheál Ó Súilleabháin describes Ó Riada as attempting to 'breathe life' into the harp music through the harpsichord.

For *Bringing It All Back Home*, Mícheál recorded on harpsichord a harp composition by Carolan, called 'Fanny Poer'. It was, he says, a favourite piece of Ó Riada's (featured on the *Ó Riada's Farewell* album). 'He used to play it with certain variations in the baroque style, and I borrowed some of these and put in some of my own.'

This rehabilitation of an ancient tradition goes on. Attempts to reconstruct wire-strung Irish harps have been successful and there are harpers very interested in learning how to play them in the old style. Mícheál Ó Súilleabháin is hopeful about the future of the Irish harp:

> *Since the 1970s in particular there are waves of very young passsionate harpers around the country, and indeed outside Ireland experimenting daily with techniques....*
>
> *I think ultimately what we're all waiting for is a new generation of Irish harpers who are going somehow or other to link back into that original broken spark in the early nineteenth century; and that can only come through a new kind of creativity.*

There are some striking parallels between Ó Riada and Carolan. Both had a foot in two worlds, that of an endangered traditional music culture, and that of the literate art-music tradition. Both were outstanding composers in both idioms, and both brought the two worlds closer together.

IRISH TRADITIONAL MUSIC AND EUROPEAN ART MUSIC

Ó Riada's film scores in the sixties had combined traditional and European art music to new effect. According to Gerard Victory, Ó Riada's achievement was 'to translate the authentic inflection to symphonic terms'.

Previous arrangements of traditional music had, with some honourable exceptions, often been dull and out of sympathy with the spirit of the music. They also smacked of cultural tokenism, a gesture in the direction of the 'native' culture, forced upon composers and arrangers. Ó Riada broke with this practice and showed other composers and arrangers the possibilities of combining the two idioms.

This is all the more noteworthy when his other compositions are taken into account. Ó Riada was himself a serious composer of modern European art music, and produced four significant works in this idiom, 'Hercules Dux Ferrariae' for string orchestra, two choral works 'Five Greek Epigrams' and 'Nomos No. 2', and the 'Hölderlin Songs' for voice and piano. Of 'Hercules'

I firmly believe his [Ó Riada's] eventual goal was to attempt the synthesis of his new traditional art with European music.
GERARD VICTORY[7]

7 Gerard Victory, 'Ó Riada on Radio. Integrating Tradition', *The Achievement of Seán Ó Riada*, p. 58

Gerard Victory says:

> *Although 'Hercules' betrays little evidence of the melodic contours we associate with Irish music, it is unmistakably the work of a great Irishman and could have been written by no one else. The type of imagination which informs it with its peculiar blend of real scholarship ... with irony even cynicism and almost perverse gaiety is unmistakably Irish.*[8]

MÍCHEÁL Ó SÚILLEABHÁIN

Mícheál Ó Súilleabháin now occupies a position in the Department of Music in University College Cork, where Seán Ó Riada once taught. Mícheál has continued the work begun by Ó Riada, 'interfacing' traditional and European art music. *Bringing It All Back Home* recorded two of Mícheál's recent works, the second movement of the 'Oileán/Island' composition and 'Idir Eatharu/Between Worlds'.

'Oileán/Island' is a work for traditional flute and chamber orchestra in three movements. For this recording the flute was played by John McCarthy, a musician from Cork, whom Mícheál describes as 'bi-musical'. John teaches classical flute, but also plays traditional music on the wooden flute. This is an unusual combination but neither impinges on the other. It is the musical equivalent of perfect bilingualism. The flute part in 'Oileán/Island' does not demand musical literacy and traditional musicians with no knowledge of music notation have also played the part.

'Oileán/Island' emerged from a commissioned work 'Concerto for Traditional Musician and String Orchestra' which Mícheál wrote in 1979. The traditional musician whom Mícheál chose to take part was flute player, Matt Molloy, now a member of The Chieftains.

The orchestral part was written to 'create a fabric around Matt's playing', using music in Matt's repertoire.

In the meantime the three-movement piece developed into 'Oileán', with a second movement consisting entirely of original music. Here the flute line is slow and moody. The atmosphere is dark, the ominous swelling strings elaborate the sombre theme. The traditional musician is given the space to exploit the full vocabulary of ornamentation within the piece, once the bar line divisions are observed.

8 Ibid., p.53

'Oileán' is the Irish for island and Mícheál found the 'Oileán/Island' title evocative and multi-layered, although the work was not composed as programme music.

There is the relationship between Ireland and England, both islands, out of which such music is made possible. Mícheál was also struck by the island images of Ireland in Seamus Heaney's trilogy of poems 'Triptych' in his *Fieldwork* collection and in a poem of the Irish-language poet, Nuala Ní Dhomhnaill. There is a dialogue in the music between two musical forms, representing two cultures.

The second work 'Idir Eatharu/Between Worlds' reiterates these dualities but in a lighthearted way. The basis of the piece is a traditional English song tune 'Jockey to the Fair' which came into Irish traditional music as a single jig. The tune is lively and exuberant as befits a good dance melody. The change from jig to hornpipe adds to the feeling of gaiety as do the traditional percussion and rhythms provided by Tommy Hayes on bodhrán and bones. The string orchestra is used to great effect to fill in the colour and tone of both pieces.

Mícheál has not to date worked with a full symphony orchestra. He considers the wooden-bodied instruments of a chamber orchestra a more organic medium for traditional music. His affinity with baroque music directs him away from 'all that colour' of the full orchestra.

SHAUN DAVEY

'All that colour' attracts composer Shaun Davey. In 1980 he composed a suite 'The Brendan Voyage' for uilleann pipes and symphony orchestra which has since taken a place in the Irish orchestral repertoire.

The work describes the voyage of an Irish saint, Brendan the Navigator, who is recorded as having sailed to America in a leather boat in the sixth century. Davey was inspired by the recreation of that voyage undertaken by the sailor, Tim Severin, who successfully established the possibility if not probability of such a journey.

Davey was struck by the way in which Severin's account of the contemporary voyage 'describes various meeting points between mediæval and modern culture'. He was drawn to explore the common terrain on which 'old and contemporary music' might meet.

The 'Brendan Voyage' consists of ten parts, each of which describes episodes of the voyage and in which the pipes represent the boat. The piper who performed the part was Liam O'Flynn. Since the 'Brendan Voyage' Shaun Davey and Liam have worked together on other compositions involving orchestra and pipes. Nothing in Liam's background as a traditional musician had prepared him for performing with the wide canvas of sound produced by a full orchestra. When he became accustomed to it he found 'the sheer size of it was exhilarating'. He learnt to anticipate the playing of the orchestra and he also improved his music reading skills, to extend his understanding of the score. Within the melody line provided for him he can ornament and decorate in the traditional way without interfering with the flow of the music. While he still functions as a solo traditional piper, he enjoys and looks forward to every new experience of performing with orchestras.

CATHERINE ENNIS AND LIAM O'FLYNN

Catherine Ennis is an organist who was born and educated in England, and went on to Oxford to take a music degree. Her father was the late Seamus Ennis, a renowned music collector, broadcaster, and great uilleann piper. He married and later separated from Catherine's mother when she was four years old and it wasn't until the end of his life that she met and got to know her father again. In the meantime she had become a classically trained church organist, but was captivated by her father's music when she met him again.

For *Bringing It All Back Home* Catherine played one of her father's favourite pieces, 'Easter Snow', with uilleann piper Liam O'Flynn. She and Liam have recorded together in the past; Liam was taught by her father and now plays his pipes. He too learned 'Easter Snow' from Seamus. The combination of organ and pipes is unusual. Catherine loves the effect: 'I think they sound very mystical together because the pipes sound like an extension of the organ; it's like having a stop, but a sort of human stop rather than just a series of organ pipes. It's a living sort of vibrato beautifully ornamented stop.'

ROARATORIO

Traditional music has had many encounters by now with non-traditional music. One of the strangest has been with the 'Roaratorio', the work of American composer, John Cage. It is not correct to describe this music as western art music since John Cage is an avant-garde composer who has abandoned all

Catherine as a child, with her father, piper Seamus Ennis. Catherine is now a professional organist

the fundamental precepts of art-music composition.

The work is a soundscape based on *Finnegan's Wake* by James Joyce, in which traditional music, text, and tape-recordings are interwoven. The recordings are of sounds which are mentioned in the book. These are multi-tracked to give the effect of a river of sound which runs continually through the performance. John Cage meanwhile intones 'mesostics' or word formations which he constructs from the text of *Finnegan's Wake*.

While all this is going on, six traditional musicians perform, at will, any piece of music they wish, provided their whole contribution is not longer than twenty minutes. None of the traditional performances is in any way co-ordinated. 'Roaratorio' is a 'sound experience' rather than a work in the orthodox way. It expresses John Cage's preoccupation with the need to break down the barriers between music and the impositions (as he sees them), placed on it by formal constructions such as harmony and metre. This makes music artificial and exclusive.

The sounds of life, and the contingency of life should be represented in music. In Cage's view, *Finnegan's Wake* which dispenses with formal narrative and linguistic structures corresponds with his philosophy of music composition.

'Roaratorio' has not received many performances since it was written but *Bringing It All Back Home* was lucky to be able to film a performance in Huddersfield in November 1989. On this occasion the six traditional performers were Liam Ó Flynn (uilleann pipes), Paddy Glackin (fiddle), Seamus Tansey (flute), Peadar and Mel Mercier (bodhráns) and Nóirín Ní Riain (singer).

Initially the traditional musicians thought 'Roaratorio' mad, hare-brained, or worse. In the end, however, they came to respect and admire Cage's vision, and all of them enjoy the rare opportunity to play at a performance. As Peadar Mercier commented on the programme:

> *At first I thought it was dreadful – utterly dreadful balderdash, but as time went on I began to listen and I gradually fell in love with the thing.... Everyone in life has something to look forward to; their holidays or to go fishing or whatever; and what I look forward to most ... is another Roaratorio.... It's marvellous to think that something that to me was ugly at the outset now stands as a little joy in my life.*[9]

THE ROAD AHEAD

More and more opportunities are becoming available for traditional and 'classical' music to come together. An important breakthrough was recognition by the music department of University College Cork of the value of oral traditional music. Since 1980 musical literacy is no longer a necessary requirement for admission to the degree course. The UCC course increases in popularity every year and the ratio of traditional to non-traditional musician is now one in three. This bodes well for the future. At the very least it means that the understanding that both traditions have for each other is expanded.

> *Well at the moment the future looks very exciting. One of the healthiest things and one of the things that many of us are happy about is that the mainstream, so-called amateur music making river of sound is still intact. There are musicians everywhere.*[10]

9 Peadar Mercier.

Interview, *BIABH*

10 Mícheál Ó Súilleabháin.

Interview, *BIABH*

INDEX